We may live without poetry, music and art

We may live without conscience, live without heart

We may live without friends

We may live without books

But civilised man cannot live without cooks.

"Keep the Dream Alive"

John Lawson.

JOHN LAWS'
BARBECUE
COOKBOOK

First published 1996 in Macmillan by
Pan Macmillan Australia Pty Limited
St Martins Tower, 31 Market Street, Sydney
Produced by Lansdowne Publishing Pty Ltd
Sydney, Australia

National Library of Australia
cataloguing-in-publication data:

Laws, John, 1935–
John Laws' barbecue cookbook.

Includes index.
ISBN 0 7329 0868 X.

1. Barbecue cookery. I. Title.
II. Title: Barbecue cookbook.
641.5784

Typeset in Courier on QuarkXpress
Printed in Australia by McPherson's Printing Group

Recipe Consultant: Margaret Gore

Photography
Thanks to: John Hollingshead, Photographer
Kay Francis, Stylist
Margaret McDonagh, Home Economist
Bed, Bath n' Table, Mosman NSW
Kitchen Kapers, Crows Nest NSW
Neil Ayres Top Grade Meats, North Sydney NSW

Page 2: Budget Hamburger, recipe page 32;
Barbecued Potatoes, recipe page 150

CONTENTS

FOREWORD

I call Australia God's great garden. And it is. We grow the best of everything. Sometimes, sadly, we export the best and keep the second-best. But even the second-best, for my money, is better than the rest.

We have the most wonderful climate, the cleanest environment and we produce the most superb foodstuff. And not just foodstuff, drinkstuff too. Our wines compare with the best in the world and some, in fact, are the best in the world. Tasmania must never be forgotten for not only creating extraordinarily good foodstuff, but now extraordinarily good wines as well. There'll be more about wine further into the book.

Recently I saw Australian wines described as 'easy to drink'. When it comes to eating I feel a bit the same way about barbecued food; not only is it easy to eat but it's easy to prepare. And this is one circumstance in which too many cooks can never spoil the broth — even though it would be rare to be cooking broth on a barbecue, but not impossible, because virtually nothing is impossible with the barbecue.

The thing that perhaps most people love about the barbecue is the feeling of festivity, the inclusion of lots of people. All can be involved but individuals can cook their steak the way they like it, or turn their chop when they want. They can stab their sausage, they can stuff it, they can slice it and they can serve it. Barbecues have many beauties, these are just some. Barbecues are the ultimate in fuss-free food.

This book couldn't have been created without the help of my many listeners around Australia and also quite a number of the restaurants that I have visited around the country made contributions for which I am very grateful. The book also contains recipes supplied by the Australian Meat and Livestock Corporation with whom I am proud to have an association. This is yet another venture in which I wanted the people who have been so loyal to me over the years to be involved. They have been part of my radio broadcasts for more years than I intend to admit, and they have become part of my life, so I want them now to be part of my ventures — whether it's creating a calendar, making a record or producing a barbecue book. Without them, this book would not have been done and certainly not with the enthusiasm I hope you will discover between the covers. And I want you to know that if you feel improvements could be made or if you've come up with a better recipe, don't throw it away. Send it to me, because if the response was to continue the way it has for the first book, volume after volume might become available. In any case, even if some of the recipes don't work for you, or are not quite what you expected, the main thing is that you've been together with your family, your friends, and you've had a festivity in the form of something I believe is true blue Australian ... the barbecue.

I think that the delight Australians take in barbecuing goes back to our heritage of being fundamentally 'free'. We like open spaces because there was a time, of course, when that was all we had. If you can, get out into the bush with some Carlton Cold (that's super cold) or some Light Ice if you are driving home, some fine Australian wine, some great Australian cheese like Wauchope Gloucester or better still Hunter Valley Cheeses, King Island brie or cheddar (towards the back of the book I have included a list of my favourite cheeses), big hunks of bread and big cuts of beef. What more could you ask for? If you can only make it as far as your own backyard, you can make it a little fancier. Add some crispy bacon, vegetables, kebabs, even roasts if you have the right kind of barbecue — in fact, you can damn nearly do whatever you like.

What we put on the barbecue has certainly changed over the years. But, for my money, there's still nothing like a superb lean piece of the finest beef in the world, grown here in Australia, or a double cut chop, twice as thick, twice as juicy, trimmed of fat, and as healthy as anything you can eat. Now of course we include chicken and fish to a greater extent — and why not barbecued fish? We have some of the best in the world. What other country can boast a barramundi? None, I am telling you. None.

These days we create marinades and special flavourings. But no matter what we do, no matter how we try and move it up-market, the great Australian barbecue is still just that — the great Australian barbecue. It's very hard to go wrong. Whether you're using real wood that you pick up around your campsite and bust over your knee, or bits of bark, gum leaves, charcoal (it's coming in better value bags these days), gas (the purist might object but it's good and it works), or even electric (the purist will really turn their back on that but there are lots available), there are plenty of options. Now we've got good barbecues with lids so you can actually roast a piece of lamb. You can even bake a cake if you want! But that's not for me — I'm into basic barbecuing.

Whatever you do, cook big food — no wishy-washy, dainty little dishes — good, strong, big food. Barbecues are not about being delicate. In the great outdoors food tends to lose its flavour and people seem to gain their appetite, so stick with good, gutsy, strong-flavoured foods and you won't go wrong. But don't forget the liquid refreshment!

My barbecuing days started in the bush with a 44-gallon drum cut longways, some wire mesh over the top (sometimes we even used an old wire door mat), and an old plough disc which was terrific because it had a drain hole in the middle. If you do it the right way, nobody can destroy that authentic Australian outdoor feast, and that's what it should be.

All of my barbecuing these days, of course, is done on the barbecues that I designed and we have recently marketed Australia wide through Barbeques Galore. The lowest priced one is called the Fair Dinkum 44, a charcoal barbecue that I wanted to be about as close as I could get to the old 44-gallon drum. The results are terrific. Then there's one we call the Knockabout — for obvious reasons. It's a plate, it's gas, and it's terrific if you're having a whole bunch of people who can do their own barbecuing in their own time.

The top of the line model is the Dream, which is wonderful as it's as good as having a proper oven outdoors. Consequently it's a lot more versatile — you can do the most wonderful roasts — because you've got the benefits of indirect cooking. That simply means hot air is circulating around the food, no heat is actually underneath it. This means cooking is slightly slower because there's less heat but there's also virtually no possibility of flare up from dripping fat. You can use this method whenever you feel inclined — some people like to use it for barbecues, but that's up to you. You'll find this information and more in the instruction book for your own barbecue.

Just before we get on with the cooking, let me make a couple of suggestions concerning some other essentials that I've learned over years of experience. It's a great idea to take an insect repellant with you. The one I use is called Off Skintastic. It's not an aerosol can, it's pump action and the little bottle fits easily in your breast pocket or your handbag — try not to forget it because it is important. Another sensible thing to have is a big, strong, long, oven glove — and as men get involved with much of the barbecuing, you have to have a big size. But be warned: I've had hell's own job trying to get one big enough to fit my hand after the glove is washed — they all seem to shrink. I've finally found one sold in Australia, the Pyrotex Flameguard oven mit. It's made from a special wipe-clean fabric that doesn't need washing.

I hope you get pleasure from the recipes in this book, but more than that, I hope you get pleasure from the barbecue. I've always had great admiration for a man who had the ability to be a sitter by a fire and I still believe that in all my life some of the best times have been doing just that — sitting by the fire doing just what was necessary at the time. We live in a big country, there's so much space and so much room for all. We can all fly with the birds, float with the clouds because the openness of Australia allows you to be part of it — free. And whether you take your barbecue and your barbecue book and head for the hills as I often say, or whether you sit in your own back garden, smelling the smells, hearing the sounds, tasting the flavours, feeling the friendship — remember that sitting around a campfire is the foundation of much of this country, and perhaps the foundation of the Australian attitude. The barbecue to me is the great leveller. It matters little how much money you have, how much material wealth you may possess — the richest man in the country, I doubt, could make a better fire on a better barbecue than the one I hope you will be enjoying soon.

BARBECUING BASICS

Barbecues come in all shapes and sizes — from small portable hibachis to the average backyard gas trolley barbecue, from brick constructions to custom-built barbies which house not only a hot plate and grill but also a roasting hood, rotisserie, warming rack and gas burners for saucepans or woks.

The type of barbecue which is right for you depends on the space available, your budget, the style of food you like to cook, the number of people you usually serve and how often you intend to barbecue. A couple living in a town house who don't entertain much would only need a simple barbecue, while a family who love having guests would need a larger trolley or built-in style.

Here is an outline of the different types of barbecues available and some handy hints on how to get the best from them.

Hibachi

This is a simple brazier usually made from cast iron. Its Japanese name means "fire bowl" and that's just what it is — a metal bowl in which charcoal is burned. An adjustable metal grid sits above the bowl to hold the food. It's ideal for use on balconies and in courtyards and is just fine for cooking steaks, chops, sausages, fish fillets and kebabs.

The standard portable barbecue

This consists of a simple metal bowl, supported by three, detachable metal legs, with an adjustable grid above it. Some styles come with a shield which is positioned into the wind to shelter the coals and maintain the right cooking temperature. They can be fuelled by charcoal or gas. Battery-operated or manual rotisseries are an optional extra with this style.

When buying a portable barbecue make sure it's made from quality materials and is well supported on sturdy legs — you don't want it to tip over in the wind halfway through cooking lunch.

Trolley barbecues

Ideal when cooking for a crowd, these barbecues have large working areas either side of the cooktop and a shelf below for holding the gas cylinder and accessories. Fuelled by gas or electricity which heats up volcanic lava rock in trays beneath the cooktop, they often have two cooking surfaces — one an open grill, the other a solid hot plate — so you can even cook fried eggs and pancakes. This style sometimes comes with a roasting hood, which allows a greater variety of cooking techniques as it helps retain the heat and juices. Covered cooking also cuts approximately two-thirds of the cooking time compared to open grilling and saves on gas usage.

Kettle barbecues

A kettle barbecue is like having a conventional oven in the garden, only better because it can also be used for smoking food. Round or square with a hinged or removable lid, they can be made of steel plate or cast aluminium and can have a variety of finishes, including enamel, stainless steel, or paint. A kettle barbecue is more versatile than a standard hoodless barbecue as it also allows you to roast, bake, braise and stew food.

Kettle barbecues can be fuelled by charcoal or, more commonly these days, by products such as Heat Beads or Hot Shots. Easy to use, you can cook some great tasting meals in them, even a traditional roast turkey dinner (see the recipe in this book), so no more slaving over a hot stove on Christmas Day!

Fuels

Gas, electricity, charcoal and wood can be used for barbecuing — so long as the fuel burns hot enough, it has little effect on flavour (unless you are smoking the food).

Gas is an inexpensive fuel for the barbecue and, unlike other fuels, has the advantage of being instantly available at the temperature you require. Gas cylinders come in all shapes and sizes to suit your needs — some more portable than others — and can be refilled at service stations, barbecue specialists and camping stores.

Electric barbecues have to be plugged into a power source so they are either a built-in feature of the garden connected to the mains supply, or a trolley style with an extension lead from the house. Take care when using the trolley barbies so that no accidents occur, such as someone tripping over the cord.

Charcoal, in briquette or lump form, is really quite portable, making it ideal for both picnics and home use. Bags of charcoal are available from service stations, supermarkets, barbecue specialists and camping stores. Charcoal, however, takes some time to heat to the right cooking temperature. You can generally tell if it's ready for cooking during the day when the coals turn an ashy white all over; at night they should be glowing red all over.

When using wood, build a good fire, then let it die down until the coals become ashy white (by day), or turn to glowing embers (by night).

Before you begin cooking

• Wash and wipe hot plate before using and lightly brush it with oil.
• Heat the barbecue well before cooking — this may take only 5-10 minutes for gas but up to 1 hour for charcoal or wood. This way, you make sure that your meat sears and that food such as seafood cooks quickly.

- Covered barbecues should always be open when you light them.
- Always thaw meat before barbecuing to ensure the inside cooks without the outside overcooking.
- Use marinades to tenderise meat — a mixture that combines a seasoning and oil with an acidic ingredient (like lemon juice, vinegar or wine) is best. Fish only needs about an hour or two to marinate as it is fine-fleshed and also absorbs flavours easily.
- When using bamboo skewers, soak them in water for 30 minutes to stop them burning while cooking. If using metal skewers, oil them well before use so that it's easy to remove food once it is cooked.

General cooking tips

- *Direct cooking* is simply when the food is placed directly over the heat, whether it's on an open grill or a hotplate (even if the food is wrapped in foil). It's the traditional way of barbecuing. *Indirect cooking* is cooking without a direct heat source under the food. The food is cooked by the heat of the air (preheated like an oven) and is now possible with hooded barbecues which let you roast, bake, smoke and steam. Sausages are great cooked in is way.
- A point to remember when barbecuing is that although it may be spectacular to cook over flame, the most effective way is to use radiant heat from the coals.
- Always sear meat over high heat for a few minutes each side to trap in the juices; then move it to a cooler part of the barbecue or raise the level of the grid and continue cooking to taste.
- You can cook fish unscaled then, once it's cooked, peel off the skin and scales. This seals in the moisture and flavour. Fish can also be cooked inside special metal grids or baskets.
- If wrapping food in foil to cook, place the dull side to the outside and the shiny side inside.
- Use oil and oil-based mixtures as bastes during cooking. Bastes of water or stock will only evaporate and toughen meat. If using bastes containing sugar, jam or honey, apply them towards the end of cooking and watch them carefully as sweet mixtures scorch easily.
- Spit roasting cooks meat in its own juices. The meat should be balanced securely on the rotisserie so that when it turns the top of the meat moves towards the back of the barbecue. Always place a drip tray on the grid under the meat to stop fat dripping into the coals and causing flare-ups. The tray can contain water, red wine or beer to give extra flavour as the liquid steams.
- Meat benefits from resting before slicing. The flesh relaxes and becomes more tender and the tasty juices develop. If you cover it loosely with foil before setting aside, it won't get cold.

How long does it take?

Timing will depend on the characteristics of your own barbecue and the heat you are using as much as the size of the piece of food. These times are guides only. Keep a close eye on your food and test it as soon as you think it's done. Overcooking can spoil a well-prepared meal.

- For beef steaks, Trim Lamb steaks and lamb cutlets:
  First, sear for 2–3 minutes each side, then
  Rare — remove immediately after searing
  Medium — move to a cooler part of the barbecue and continue cooking for a further 2–3 minutes each side
  Well done — move to a cooler part of the barbecue and continue cooking for a further 4–6 minutes each side.
- For Trim Lamb eye of loin, eye fillets and loin chops:
  Seal for 4–5 minutes each side and then:
  Rare — remove immediately after sealing
  Medium — move to a cooler part of the barbecue and continue cooking for a further 2–3 minutes each side
  Well done — move to a cooler part of the barbecue and continue cooking for a further 4–6 minutes each side.
- For chicken fillets:
  Cook about 4–5 minutes each side, depending on thickness.
- For chicken joints with bone:
  Cook 8–10 minutes each side, depending on size.
- For whole fish:
  Allow 20–25 minutes cooking time per kilo.
- For fish fillets, cutlets and steaks:
  Allow 4–5 minutes each side, depending on thickness, turning only once. Cooking time can also vary according to type of fish as well as size.
- For shellfish:
  Cook over medium heat for the following times —
  Mussels 6 minutes (discard any that do not open)
  Prawns 3–5 minutes
  Scallops 2 minutes
  Balmain bugs 5–6 minutes per side
  Lobster 5–8 minutes per side

To test if food is cooked

- Beef, lamb, pork and veal — don't cut into meat to see if it is cooked because the juices will escape and the meat toughen. Do the touch test instead. Using tongs, press the meat; rare should feel soft to the touch; medium will have a little resistance; well done will be firm. It's also a good idea to use a meat thermometer for larger pieces of meat, so you can accurately tell the stage of cooking that has been reached.

They are inexpensive and readily available from the cooking sections of department stores, and Barbeques Galore.
• Chicken — pierce the thickest part of the meat with a skewer. If the juices run pink, then continue cooking.
• Seafood — fish is cooked when the flesh flakes easily with a fork. The flesh should just become opaque. Shellfish should be cooked quickly as it becomes tough when overcooked.

Accompaniments
If space allows, you can cook the whole meal on a barbecue.
• You can steam vegetables in covered foil trays on top of the grid. Simply cut the vegetables into bite-size pieces, place into foil trays, sprinkle over about $1/4$ cup water and seal tightly with foil. Dense vegetables, like potatoes and pumpkin will take about 40–45 minutes, softer vegetables like zucchinis will take about 10–15 minutes.
• Alternatively, brush vegetables with oil and roast them in foil trays on top of the grid. Turn and baste with oil frequently. They will take about 45–60 minutes.
• To cook vegetables in a kettle barbecue use the indirect heat method: place vegetables such as potatoes, pumpkin etc directly onto the upper grill and cover with the hood (refer to the manufacturer's instructions for specific direction on this type of cooking in your barbecue).
• Why not place a wok on the hottest part of the barbecue and quickly stir-fry vegetables? The meat or fish can stand, covered with foil while you do this. You can also use a wok to quickly cook instant noodles on the barbecue for a tasty accompaniment.
• Cook jacket potatoes in the coals by piercing the skin in a few places, brushing with oil, then wrapping in heavy duty foil. Place in the coals and cook for 45–60 minutes, turning occasionally. Individual portions of other vegetables can also be cooked in this way.
• Make tasty bread on the barbecue by slicing a French stick, spreading both sides with garlic/herb butter, reforming the loaf and wrapping it in heavy duty foil. Place in the coals or on the barbecue grid, turning occasionally, for 8–10 minutes until heated through.

After cooking
• If using gas, turn up high for approximately 10 minutes after cooking to burn away excess fat. Make sure the hood is open.
• Turn off gas first, then the controls.
• Let your barbecue cool slightly, scrape off any food. Wipe clean.
• Lightly coat cast-iron surfaces with oil after cleaning as this will prevent rusting.
• When barbecue is cool, cover with a fitted vinyl cover.

Beef cuts

The quality and tenderness of your beef will depend not only on the cut but on the sex, age and condition of the animal and how well it has been handled (hard things to know at the supermarket!). The rump and loin produces the most tender meat. Rump (which is boneless) is recommended for barbecuing as is sirloin steak or T-bone (which also comes from the sirloin area). Porterhouse, cut from the sirloin and containing a piece of fillet, is another quality cut. Boneless topside (the inside part of the butt) and round (from the front of the butt) can be marinated before barbecuing, as can even cheaper cuts such as blade (oyster, cross-cut or yearling). From the ribs, you can get rib steak (which has the bone in), rib eye (or Scotch) fillet, and the spare ribs (the part left over after the eye meat is removed) — all are great on the barbecue.

Lamb cuts

Lamb is at its very best during spring. Chump chops are the main choice of cut for the barbecue, but a leg of lamb can also be cooked if you have a hooded barbecue. You can roast the whole leg, on the bone or boned. Otherwise, use a butterflied leg — where the bone has been removed and the meat laid flat. This can be marinated and cooked on any barbecue, although it can also be stuffed and roasted.

BEEF

Barbecued Steak

Serves 4

4 t-bone or sirloin steaks
2 tablespoons oil
salt and pepper to taste

1. Cut away any fat to prevent flare-up while cooking. Brush steak with oil and season to taste with salt and pepper.
2. Set a gas or electric barbecue to high. If using charcoal or wood, build a good fire, then let it die down until the coals turn white.
3. For a perfect barbecue steak, the meat needs to be sealed well to retain its juiciness. Seal steak on one side over high heat for 2-3 minutes or until juices appear on the uncooked side. Turn over and seal the other side for 2-3 minutes. If you like your steak rare, remove immediately. If you like your steak medium, move meat to a cooler part of the barbecue and continue cooking for a further 2-3 minutes each side. For well done, cook for a further 4-6 minutes each side after sealing.
4. Test if steak is done by pressing with tongs. Rare is soft to touch, medium has a little resistance and well done feels firm. Don't cut into steak to see if it is cooked because you will lose tasty juices.

Szechuan Peppercorn Steaks

A friend of mine recently introduced me to Szechuan peppercorns. Get some Szechuan peppercorns (green and white peppercorns) and prepare yourself a barbecued pepper steak.

Mix one teaspoon of each colour of peppercorns together and crush them.

Take the fat off the steak, as usual (I used sirloin for this but you can use rump). Press the mixed crushed peppercorns into both sides of the steak — firmly — use a meat cleaver (any flat implement would do). Then on the hot plate of your barbecue melt a little unsalted butter. When it's melted and the hot plate is not sticky, put the steak on but treat it with caution because you don't want too many peppercorns to fall off. And only turn it once, because if you turn it often the peppercorns *will* fall off and the flavour will go. If you want it rare (let's say it's about three-quarters or one inch thick), cook for $2^1/_2$ to 3 minutes on each side), about 4 to $4^1/_2$ minutes for medium, about 7 minutes for well-done meat.

When it's cooked put it on a cold plate, that helps the juices run out. Put a slab of unsalted butter on top and if, you like, sprinkle some chives or chopped parsley on top of the butter … it tastes wonderful.

See picture on page 19.

Robyn's Marinated Meat

Ingredients –

750g Blade Steak
75ml Vinegar
1 tab sp Worchestireshire Sauce
½ tab sp HP Sauce
½ tab sp BBQ Sauce
½ tab sp Steak Sauce
½ tab sp Soy Sauce
6 drops Tabasco Sauce approx
½ tea sp Chilli Powder

Method –

Trim fat from steak.
Combine all remaining ingredients in a shallow dish.
Place meat in marinate and leave for several hours or overnight, turning meat over a few times.
BBQ meal, pouring remaining marinate over whilst cooking.

NB – quantities can be increased or reduced according to your taste

This recipe is from Mrs Robyn Scali, Collaroy Plateau, NSW.

Satay Beef

Serves 4

500 g rump steak, cut into bite-size pieces
$1/2$ cup coconut cream
4 shallots, finely chopped
1 clove garlic, crushed
1 tablespoon soy sauce
1 tablespoon fish sauce
1 red chilli, seeded and chopped
2 stalks lemongrass, finely chopped
1 teaspoon honey
$1/2$ teaspoon ground cumin
bamboo skewers, soaked in water for 30 minutes
$1/2$ cup peanut butter
$1/4$ cup coconut cream, extra
1 tablespoon soy sauce, extra
2 teaspoons lemon juice
1 teaspoon grated fresh ginger

1. Place the steak in a bowl. Combine the coconut cream, shallots, garlic, soy sauce, fish sauce, chilli, lemongrass, honey and cumin in a bowl. Pour over meat and mix well to coat evenly. Cover and refrigerate for at least 4 hours, or overnight.
2. Drain meat and reserve marinade. Thread meat onto skewers. Brush with marinade and barbecue over medium heat for 4–5 minutes each side or until cooked to taste, basting with marinade while cooking.
3. Meanwhile, place the peanut butter in a saucepan with the coconut cream, extra soy sauce, lemon juice and ginger. Heat to boiling point then simmer, stirring, for 2 minutes.
4. Serve with the beef satays accompanied by steamed rice and side dishes of cucumber and yoghurt, and banana and coconut

Right: Satay Beef (top left); Szechuan Peppercorn Steaks, recipe page 16

A Light-weight Barbecue

The reason for the name is that the steak is sliced very thinly across the grain from the top to the bottom. So you get a hunk of sirloin or a hunk of rump, slice some off thinly, but across the grain. Let's give you the recipe that will feed four people.

The important thing about this is the marinade and, of course, the quality of the beef, although it's hard to get bad quality beef in Australia. Specify you want it lean, it must be lean. You can use the skirt steak I talk about in the hamburger recipe (see page 31) if you're a little strapped, or rib, sirloin or rump.

Ingredients
1 kg steak (semi-frozen makes slicing easier)
3 or 4 finely chopped chives
4 or 5 garlic cloves (depending how much you
   like garlic)
1 tbsp sesame seeds
2 tbsps sesame oil
sherry (optional — it is nice, however, especially
      sweet sherry or Tio Pepe)
black pepper
soy sauce
That ought to do it.

Slice the steak very thinly. Combine all the other ingredients in a bowl, mix up this marinade, and pop it in a processor. Spread all over the meat. Flip the meat backwards and forwards for a while until it gets totally covered. Leave the meat in the marinade for some time — I would recommend $2^1/2$ to 3 hours.

Then just take it out, throw it on the barbecue for a few minutes on each side (turn it only once) — and there you go!

Left: Barbecued Tomatoes and Onions (top), recipe page 150;
A Light-weight Barbecue (front)

Oriental Beef Sticks

Serves 4-6

750 g lean beef strips (prepared from rump or round)
1/2 cup plum sauce
2 teaspoons soy sauce
1 clove garlic, crushed
1/2 teaspoon grated fresh ginger
1/4 teaspoon minced chilli

1. Preheat barbecue on high. Weave beef strips on 8–12 oiled bamboo skewers.
2. Combine all the remaining ingredients and brush over the meat. Barbecue skewers 3–4 minutes each side, brushing repeatedly with the spicy sauce.

Cook's tips: If you like to add vegetables to your skewers, make sure the pieces are the same size as the meat. Button mushrooms and baby squash can be used whole. Fruit can work well (both for its colour and flavour), but must be firm, not overripe or soft. Onion is great on a kebab or satay. Cook a few minutes first by simmering it in water or cooking it for a minute in the microwave oven.

BBQ Carpetbag Kilpatrick Steak

Take a nice thick 250 gm scotch fillet medallion, trimmed of all visible fat. Make two vertical cuts, 2/3 way through. Pull each of the three sections a little apart, cut small pocket in each and stuff with a fresh oyster seasoned with lemon juice, salt and pepper. Thread steak along a skewer to hold sections together. Char-grill each side for two minutes, then finish on hotplate to required "doneness". Serve drizzled with warmed kilpatrick sauce, and Dolly's famous Caesar salad.

Kilpatrick Sauce

Mix equal amounts tomato and Worcestershire sauce. Add a little fresh garlic and a drizzle each of soy sauce and fresh lemon juice to taste.

Dolly's Famous Caesar Salad

For each person, toss a mixture of crunchy iceberg, mesclun and frillice lettuce. Add one roughly chopped egg, bacon and bread croutons to taste. Just before serving, toss lightly in caesar dressing, garnish with freshly shaved parmesan, cross two anchovies on top, and sprinkle with chopped parsley.

Caesar Dressing

To 4 litres mayonnaise add 2 cups parmesan and 1/4 cup garlic. Blend well.

Homemade mayonnaise

Separate 30 eggs. Keep whites for pavlovas. Blend in food processor then gradually add 2 litres poly-unsaturated oil (not olive), 200 ml water, 125 ml vinegar, 125 ml lemon juice.

Bacon croutons

Shred lean bacon quite finely. Place in baking tray and bake in moderate oven, tossing frequently until it is well browned. Drain very well in strainer, or over paper towel, reserving the fat for croutons. Cool.

Bread croutons

Cube stale bread — remove burnt crusts. Toss well in mix of bacon fat, grated parmesan, garlic oil, anchovy oil and ghee. Bake, turning often till golden brown.

Now, if you really can't be bothered with all this rigmarole, just come to the Dolly Pot — either in Tennant Creek or Darwin, and let us pamper you and show you how it's done!

This recipe is from Karen Sheldon, Dolly Pot Inn Restaurant, Darwin and Tennant Creek, NT.

Beer Roast

1 x 2½ kg blade roast
1 x tin button mushrooms
1 x packet French onion soup
1 x cup beer

Place everything in camp oven. Cook on medium heat according to weight. Make gravy from juice in camp oven.

Barbecued Mince Pizza

3 bacon rashers, chopped
500 g minced steak
1 large onion, finely chopped
½ tsp paprika
½ tsp dried oregano
1 clove garlic, crushed
3 tblsp tomato paste
250 g grated mozzarella cheese
90 g sliced mushrooms
1 green capsicum, sliced
1 tomato, sliced
2 tblsp grated parmesan cheese
½ tsp dried basil

Fry bacon until crisp; drain.

Combine mince, onion, paprika, oregano and garlic. Press mixture evenly into a lamington tray. Spread evenly with tomato paste, then mozzarella cheese, bacon, mushrooms, capsicum and lastly, sliced tomato. Sprinkle with parmesan cheese and basil. Cover with foil, barbecue for 10 minutes.

Uncover, drain off juices, and barbecue until mince is cooked through, and cheese melted. Drain off juices.

These recipes are from Michelle Tabulo, Rosedale, QLD.

Sweet Chilli Herbed Roast

Serves 2

1 beef eye fillet, about 500 g
1 shallot
4 fresh mint leaves
1 large clove garlic, peeled and quartered
1 tablespoon chopped fresh coriander
1 tablespoon sweet chilli sauce
1 tablespoon canola oil

1. Prepare an indirect fire in a covered barbecue.
2. Cut a pocket through length of roast by running a sharp knife from one end to the other. Cut shallot to length of pocket, and insert along with the mint leaves and garlic.
3. Combine coriander, chilli sauce and oil in a large dish. Add meat and turn to coat in the marinade. Leave in a cool place for 30 minutes.
4. Cook roast over drip tray for 25-30 minutes, brushing with marinade throughout cooking. Leave, covered, for 5-10 minutes before carving.

Dear John,
I'm thrilled you love my
recipe so much! Enjoy.
With love
Lyndey x

Thai Beef Salad

An alternative to carpaccio, this recipe is absolutely up-to-date — an extremely economical use of beef. It is also quick to prepare and presents well on the plate. It can be served either as an entree, or with a green salad as a main course.

500 g rump steak (trimmed of fat) or eye fillet of beef

Dressing
juice of 3-4 limes
1 tablespoon sugar syrup (or a little more to taste)
2 tablespoons Thai fish sauce (nam pla)
1 red chilli, finely chopped
fresh mint and coriander, chopped

Either grill your rump steak, or seal the eye fillet well in butter in a frying pan. Keep it rare. Cool and slice thinly (partially freezing the meat makes it easier). Marinate in the dressing. Serve with lettuce leaves and the following salad.

Salad
cherry tomatoes, halved
Lebanese cucumbers, finely sliced
Spanish onions, finely diced
mint leaves
coriander leaves
2 or more hot chillies (depending on your taste!), finely chopped

Mix together. Serves 10 as an entree, 6 as a main course with salad.

This recipe is from my good friend Lyndey Milan's book,
Plates Real Food For Fast People.

Snags on the Barbie

Serves 4

1 kg beef, pork or chicken sausages
2 tablespoons water

1. Place sausages in a foil tray with water and seal with a foil lid. Steam over medium heat on the barbecue for 10 minutes. Drain and pat dry.
2. Place a foil drip tray in the coals under the barbecue grid. Barbecue sausages over medium/low heat, turning frequently, for 10-15 minutes or until cooked through.
3. Serve in hot dog rolls, or with salad or potato salad and a selection of mustards.

Steak Sandwich

Serves 4

60 g butter, softened
1 tablespoon Dijon mustard
1 teaspoon Worcestershire sauce
4 minute steaks
1 avocado
1 tablespoon lemon juice
salt and pepper to taste
8 slices wholemeal bread, toasted and buttered
8 cooked king prawns

1. Combine the butter, mustard and Worcestershire sauce in a bowl. Smear over the steaks. Barbecue on a lightly oiled hot plate until juices appear on the uncooked side. Turn over and continue cooking for a further 2-3 minutes or until cooked to taste.
2. Meanwhile, remove flesh from the avocado and mash with the lemon juice and salt and pepper. Spread buttered toast with avocado. Place steak on one slice of bread and top with 2 prawns. Season to taste with salt and pepper. Top with another slice of bread. Serve immediately.

Dear John,

Hope this easy recipe makes the BBQ Cookbook. The combination of oysters and sausage is really fantastic. Everybody loves them and it's so simple. Good luck with this book, I will be the first to buy one, WE ALL LOVE A BBQ.

Carpetbag Snags

Entree or main meal
Ingredients: thick sausages, oysters.

BBQ sausages until cooked.

Split them down the middle but don't cut completely through.

Place 3 or 4 oysters in split.

Serve on a serviette or folded napkin.

A recipe from Craig Chisholm and Maggi Hayne,
Coffs Harbour, NSW.

Mexican Sausages
with Chilli Beans

Serves 4

150 g cream cheese, softened
chilli sauce, to taste
8 snow peas
440 g can red kidney beans, drained
1 teaspoon ground cumin
1 ripe tomato, chopped
8 thick beef sausages
2 small carrots, thinly sliced

1. Mix the cream cheese with chilli sauce in a small bowl. Plunge the snow peas briefly in boiling water and refresh under cold, running water.
2. Place kidney beans, cumin, tomato and a little chilli sauce (optional) in a saucepan on the barbecue; heat through gently.
3. Barbecue sausages 15-20 minutes. Slit lengthwise, but not right through. Fill with cheese mixture, insert a snow pea and carrot strip in each. Serve with chilli beans.

Tropical B.B.Q. Rissoles

1 kgm mince steak
2 onions, diced
1 egg
1 small can of drained pineapple
   pieces
Pinch of salt, season to taste
Banana can be added, opp.,
   Combine all ingredients,
   make into rissoles & BBQ

(a family favorite)

Edna E Babel

Thanks to Edna Babel for this recipe.

The Humble Hamburger

This is not riveting information I am about to give you but you might find it interesting. Nine out of ten people will tell you that the hamburger originated in Hamburg, a German city. Wrong! If anything, it's something for which we can thank the Americans, who have been eating hamburgers of sorts since the turn of the century, if not before. There was a wonderful restaurant in Hollywood, well actually in Beverley Hills, called The Brown Derby. It was right opposite my favourite hotel in Beverley Hills, the Beverley Wiltshire — where I stay regularly, always in the same suite, looking up Rodeo Drive and looking right where this great restaurant used to be. Sadly it's a thing of the past, as are many great restaurants in Los Angeles, but the Brown Derby had been serving hamburgers since 1926. For those who are interested, if you're lucky enough to be in Los Angeles, go to the Beverley Wiltshire Hotel, look directly across the road and you'll see a shop, Bulgari (the Los Angeles home of the well-known Italian jeweller) and that is where the Brown Derby used to be situated. It's a sad loss. As, incidentally, is the Bistro Gardens on Cannon Drive — it closed on 27 April, 1996.

Back to the hamburger. In the early days it was just an accepted form of snack. But the hamburger obviously came into its own with the establishment of fast food outlets around the world. In the 1950s and 1960s it really took off. Originally the hamburger was made out of the less fashionable, inexpensive cuts of meat, like minced steak, and I believe that's what it should be made out of today. Cuts like blade steak and skirt steak (we'll discuss this in more detail later) are wonderful for a hamburger and, if it's minced and reasonably lean, that's important from a health point of view — and it tastes fabulous.

There will be another group of people who will tell you it's called a hamburger because it's made of ham. Well, of course, it isn't. The name was originally the Hamburg steak. During the periods of both World Wars the hamburger suddenly became the Salisbury Steak, named after some English dietitian called J.H. Salisbury. They didn't like it being called a hamburger because of the German connotation and as you know during both World Wars relationships with Germany were tense. So the hamburger became the Salisbury steak, the German sausage became the Devon sausage and the poor old German Shepherd became the Alsatian.

However, the hamburger will remain the hamburger for ever and a day. They are wonderful barbecued because you can make the rolls so crisp by throwing them on the hot grill, and you can make masses at the one time. I just love them. With a bit of imagination, they can be a great delicacy.

Budget Hamburger

If you've a lot of people coming and the budget is a bit stretched, what about a hamburger each? If done well, they're beautiful. One of the great delights of my life has been to have a hamburger in Harry's Bar in Venice, one of the most acclaimed restaurants in the world. So if it's all right for Arigo Cipriani to serve a hamburger, then it's got to be all right for us. And you can make the dollar stretch by using blade steak, (or skirt steak, it's even cheaper). The blade bone comes from the forequarter of the beast. It's a big bone but the good thing about it is that it's nice and clean. Obviously you don't buy it with the bone — the butcher bones it for you. The meat has a little fat surrounding it. Get rid of that. It also has some marbling/streaking and that's wonderful; it keeps the meat moist whilst cooking.

Get your blade steak (or skirt steak) and mince it. Buy it minced if you like, but it's fresher if you mince it yourself and better for these reasons:
(a) you know you've got a good piece of blade steak;
(b) you can trim the fat off the outside; and
(c) it's not really a problem these days with a food processor to mince (be very careful about the food processor, if you leave the meat in there too long you'll wind up with paste, not mince).

Make sure you get good bread too — not some white doughy rubbish like you get in a lot of fast food places. Get a good gutsy bread roll — I like brown bread rolls — or try a long flat loaf and break it into bits or cut it into slices. I'll give you the quantities for just one person, and if you're having five, you can multiply the ingredients by five, and so on.

Ingredients

100–110 g trimmed beef (get rid of that fat)
couple of teaspoons of finely chopped shallots
freshly chopped herbs (if you're lucky enough to
  have some growing), about one teaspoon
ground black pepper
salt
bun

Mix the beef, shallots, herbs and pepper — make it into a nice firm shape, close to the size of the bread you are using. Have the grill hot, or the plate with a little oil. Cook the hamburger on both sides until it's done to your liking, salt and pepper it and put it on the bun or bread.

Before you put the lid on your bun you might like to put some cheese on the top (maybe some King Island brie or Wauchope Gloucester tasty cheese) and a slice of tomato (maybe try and get vine-ripened tomatoes) do what you like. Mayonnaise? Well that's what they do at Harry's Bar! Or mustard (Tamworth Hot Lick is the best). Use the S&W mayonnaise (I find it easily the best) with a slice of lemon, a little chilli sauce, or chilli plum sauce even, and serve it with a roast potato.

Not difficult, not expensive, and terrific to cook as each individual can do their own. If you've got one of our Keep the Dream Alive barbecues you can put God knows how many burgers on at once — especially the Knockabout with the big hot plate — probably about 50. Make sure you cook the bread on the barbecue as it's all part of it — get the bread fairly close to the heat if you can as this makes it crusty on the outside and soft in the middle.

PS: A last word on skirt steak. It's hard to get and it can be a bit difficult if you don't deal with it properly, but if it's minced and cooked properly it can be very tasty and very juicy. But whatever you do, don't cook it slowly or it will wind up like a Michelin tyre!

See picture on page 2.

CHINOIS

Lemongrass Skewered Minced Rump Steak with Red Curry Salsa and Crispy Lotus Chips

Serves: 4

Minced Rump Steak

1 kg minced rump steak
1 tsp coriander powder
50 gm onion, finely chopped
20 gm fresh ginger, finely chopped
2 tsp curry powder
1 tbsp sugar
8 stalks lemongrass, 10 cm long

Mix all ingredients together except lemongrass stalks. Divide mixture into 10 equal portions and mould onto each lemongrass stalk. Thread onto skewers.

Red Curry Salsa

1 stalk lemongrass, finely chopped
½ Spanish (red) onion, finely diced
2 firm but ripe tomatoes, finely diced
1 bunch fresh coriander, finely chopped
4 fresh lemons
1 tsp red curry paste
to taste fish sauce

Combine lemongrass, onion, tomatoes, and coriander. Juice the lemons and mix the juice with the red curry paste and fish sauce. Blend the 2 mixtures together to create the salsa.

Grill the lemongrass skewers to your liking and top with the red curry salsa.

For the lotus chips, finely slice a fresh lotus root and deep-fry in oil 180–200°C till golden, and drain and sprinkle with salt.

This recipe is from Allan Koh, Executive Chef, Chinois Restaurant, South Yarra, VIC.

The Turkey T-bone

Ingredients

a reasonably thickly cut T-bone steak — maybe a couple of inches thick is a good start

salt — I like coarsely ground salt best
black pepper — also coarsely ground
2-3 tablespoons butter
1 tablespoon chopped fresh parsley
chopped shallots
1 cup Wild Turkey (warm) — this is the most important ingredient, obviously.

Sprinkle the salt and ground black pepper on the T-bone well in advance and allow the steak to come to room temperature. It is always important when barbecuing any meat that it's at room temperature. So many people just take it out of the fridge and belt it on the barbecue — that's not right. Allow it to reach room temperature first.

While you're grilling the steak take a cast iron flaming pan, put it on the barbecue until it's very hot. Just before you think the steak is cooked (when it's very close in other words) melt the butter in the pan with the parsley with some shallots (don't burn the butter), then put the steak in the pan and cover both sides with the butter mixture — make sure it's got plenty.

You should have warmed that Wild Turkey somewhere too. When warm, pour it over the steak and set it alight. Serve immediately with a good red.

As we've gone a little up-market here try and get hold of a bottle of Balmoral Syrah. This is a real inky, rich, very flavoursome red wine. It's not a cheap red but we have to turn ourselves loose every now and again. If you can, try it — not, however, if you've got about eight other people around who are already three sheets to the wind by testing the Turkey before you made the sauce!

Topside Roast with Bacon and Herbs

Serves 4-6

$1^1/_2$ kg topside roast
$^1/_4$ cup fresh breadcrumbs
1 rasher rindless bacon, chopped
1 shallot, finely chopped
$^1/_2$ stalk celery, finely chopped
2 tablespoons chopped fresh parsley
2 teaspoons chopped walnuts
$^1/_2$ teaspoon dried sage
salt and pepper to taste
60g butter, melted
1 tablespoon oil

1. With a sharp knife, cut a pocket horizontally in the roast. Set aside.
2. Combine the breadcrumbs, bacon, shallots, celery, parsley, walnuts and sage in a bowl. Season to taste with salt and pepper. Add the melted butter and mix well to combine.
3. Fill the pocket in the roast with the breadcrumb stuffing and close the opening with a skewer.
4. Brush beef with oil and sprinkle with salt and pepper. Barbecue over medium heat for $1^1/_2$-2 hours or until cooked through. Allow to stand for 10-15 minutes before carving.
5. Serve with baby new potatoes and creamed corn.

Right: Veal Shoulder Stuffed with Prosciutto, Capers and Lemon (front), recipe page 51; Topside Roast with Bacon and Herbs (top)

BBQ Beef Shanks
To serve 8 people

Ingredients

1 bunch celery
4 large onions
6 carrots
4 x 2 kg whole shin beef, cut in half lengthways
oil
pinch mixed herbs
2 bay leaves
10 black peppercorns
1/2 litre beef stock
375 ml madeira
750 ml apricot nectar
750 ml pineapple juice
1/2 cup brown sugar

Method

1. Roughly dice vegetables and lightly brown in a heavy large baking pan.
2. Seal shanks in a hot pan with oil.
3. Place shanks on top of bed of already browned vegetables in a large baking pan including any bone marrow from shanks.
4. Add all remaining ingredients to baking pan.
5. Cover baking pan with foil and cook in oven for 1 hour at 200°C (must be placed in preheated oven).
6. After 1 hour remove foil and return to oven. Cook shanks for another 2 hours, basting several times with baking pan juices.
7. After this 2 hour period, check meat with a fork to ensure juices from meat are clear.
8. Remove and cool at room temperature. Trim excess fat from meat when shanks are cool.
9. Have BBQ char-grill (the hot rock type is ideal) very hot. Place shanks onto BBQ and using a brush, paint several times with spicy homemade BBQ sauce until shanks are glazed and heated right through — usually 20 minutes.

This recipe is from Shanks and Steaks, Beefeater's Bistro, Albury, NSW.

Left: Veal Stuffed with Swiss Cheese and Rosemary (top right), recipe page 52; Veal Chops with Basil and Lemon (left), recipe page 53; Veal Rolls with Ham and Sage (middle), recipe page 52

Bistecca alla Fiorentina
Steak Florentine style

This is a recipe for probably the most famous of all grilled steak: Bistecca alla Fiorentina — beef steak grilled Florentine style. It really does require a T-bone steak; it just doesn't seem to work with any other. I like the steak fairly thickly cut and the fire must be very, very, very hot. If you're lucky enough to have a bit of aged beefsteak, use it, it's better. It's also, believe it or not, better if it's done on a charcoal barbecue or a wood barbecue, like the Fair Dinkum 44, rather than gas, but it can be done on either, providing, as I say, the fire is hot.

Ingredients

Black peppercorns, ground and fairly coarse. That Sellou product that I mention on page 150 is good, because you can push the spring on the grinder down to get really thickly ground peppercorns. You would think I had an interest in the Sellou Company but I assure you I haven't, I just like their product. Push the ground peppercorns into the steak on both sides. You can do it with your fingers or the back of a serving spoon.

Make the steak at least 1^{1}/$_{2}$–2 inches thick and be sure it has thawed to room temperature before you put it on the fire. You need coarse salt (try Olsson's salt — they're an Australian company over 30 years old. You can use the salt to clean the barbecue afterwards as well). Almost the most important thing is a garlic clove or two, peeled and cut.

If you are going to use charcoal or wood, make sure that there's a white ash there before you start cooking — you'll need to start your fire a bit early. Cook the steak close to the fire if you can, it should be eaten rare but it's up to you. Give it about 5 minutes on one side and then turn it over, sprinkle some of the ground salt on the side that's cooked, then cook the other side, probably 3–4 minutes, but it will be quite rare.

Wait for it to be cooked to your taste and get that garlic clove you've peeled and rub it on the bone, up and down, up and down, up and down, so you get a strong garlic aroma — the coarseness of the bone acts like a grater and gets the garlic flavour down and into the meat. Use plenty of garlic because it's wonderful, then transfer the steak to a plate — a cold plate is best. I always put a large hunk of butter on top. Obviously the better quality the meat, the better the flavour, but even that's not as important as the garlic and the melted butter. I think it's just delicious and one of the exceptional barbecue dishes.

When we're fortunate enough to take our trips to Italy this dish is always a must — but going to Italy isn't necessary. Just go out the back to the Fair Dinkum 44, get yourself a bottle of red wine: maybe a Rosemount Shiraz, maybe the Diamond Label — it's not expensive, very highly rated and a rich, gutsy, fruity, spicy, red wine. Drink a little bit of that with your Bistecca alla Fiorentina and you could be anywhere in the world. You can fake Italy if you want to (now don't tell me you don't fake anything), it's a lot of fun.

Sloppy Hamburgers

1 lb mince (beef)
1 cup self-raising flour
1 cup milk
1 cup water
1 packet chicken noodle soup mix
1 large onion, grated
some grated carrot (optional)
2 eggs

Mix all ingredients together and leave for
a few hours to soak. Mixture is very sloppy.
Scoop onto BBQ plate to cook.
(It's very yummy once cooked.)

Ivy Feuerherdt of Port Lincoln, SA provided this recipe.

Barbecued Bourbon Blade

This version of the Turkey T-bone can be done with blade steak. I call it the Barbecued Bourbon Blade. As I've said, blade steak is fairly coarse but it has got wonderful flavour. And to flame it makes it a delight. Make sure it's lean: have your butcher remove the fat, or you remove it.

Ingredients
All you need is:
the black pepper and coarse salt
mustard, try our Tamworth Hot Lick Mustard,
if you like a hot lick. Failing that, the milder mustard is available in our Country Collection.
500 g blade steak
1 cup Wild Turkey (warm)

Spread the mustard thickly on one side. Then sprinkle on the salt and push on the pepper, which will be inclined to stick to the mustard. If you want to put a little Worcestershire sauce on before the mustard that's okay, but just do one side. Put it on the barbecue — the mustard-covered side is obviously closest to the flames — and then cover the top side the same way, spreading the mustard, sprinkling the salt and pepper. Turn gently so you don't shake off all the salt and pepper. When it's cooked put it in one of those cast iron pans we talked of earlier — big heavy things. I must admit that if they're not cared for they're inclined to rust but they are worth the trouble. They're available at Barbeques Galore stores around Australia.

Pour on the warmed Wild Turkey and flame it. Before you serve the steak slice it in thin strips across the grain — it's very important that it's across the grain — and again, a nice red. Why don't you try that ever-reliable, constantly-sought-after and much-awarded Rosemount Diamond Label Cabernet Sauvignon? It won't break the bank, but it's good. The wines I recommend, I recommend obviously because I've tried them. If you prefer your own, then by all means ... it's your feast.

Tangy Beef Ribs

Preparation time: 20 minutes plus at least 3 hours marinating

Total cooking time: 15–20 minutes

Serves 4

1 kg beef ribs
$1/2$ cup tomato sauce
2 tablespoons Worcestershire sauce
2 tablespoons soft brown sugar
$1/4$ teaspoon chilli powder
1 teaspoon paprika
1 clove garlic, crushed

1. Chop ribs into serving pieces. Bring large saucepan of water to boil. Cook ribs in boiling water for 5 minutes, drain.
2. Combine tomato sauce, Worcestershire sauce, sugar, chilli powder, paprika and garlic in large bowl, mix well and add ribs. Cover and marinate in refrigerator several hours or over-night.
3. Cook ribs on hot lightly greased barbecue 10–15 minutes, brushing frequently with marinade, or until ribs are well browned and cooked through.
4. Serve with favourite vegetables or slices of grilled pineapple.

This recipe kindly supplied by Natalie Downey, Boorowa, NSW.

Steak with Fresh Tomato Chutney

Serves 4

1 kg ripe tomatoes, peeled, seeded and chopped
4 shallots, finely chopped
1 clove garlic, crushed
$1/4$ cup tomato paste
1 tablespoon soft brown sugar
1 teaspoon grated fresh ginger
$1/2$ teaspoon ground cinnamon
$1/4$ cup chopped fresh coriander
750 g rump steak
1 tablespoon oil
salt and pepper to taste

1. Place the tomatoes into a large saucepan with the shallots and garlic. Cook over medium heat for 10–15 minutes, stirring occasionally to break up tomatoes as they cook.
2. Stir in the tomato paste, sugar, ginger and cinnamon. Continue cooking for a further 5–10 minutes or until sauce reaches a thick consistency. Stir in the coriander. Pour into sterilised jars and refrigerate until ready to use. It will store for up to a week in the refrigerator.
3. Cut the steak into serving portions. Brush with oil and season to taste with salt and pepper. Barbecue over high heat for 2–3 minutes each side, or until cooked to taste (see Barbecued Steak, page 15).
4. Serve with the tomato chutney, accompanied by jacket potatoes and foil-baked corn.

Dear John,

I really enjoy your show, and I look forward to seeing your barbecue cookbook.

Here is one of my favourite recipes, I hope you like it.

P.S. I live in a pretty little country town where everybody knows everybody, could you please read one of your "country town" sayings for me. Thanks.

Marinated Beef and Vegetable Kebabs

500 grams of beef, cut into cubes

2 green or red peppers, chopped

1 large onion, chopped into square pieces

4 tomatoes, chopped into square pieces

100 grams of mushrooms, sliced

1 tablespoon of oil

kebab bamboo sticks

Marinade

1 cup of soy sauce

¼ cup of Maggi seasoning sauce

4 tablespoons of Worcestershire sauce

½ teaspoon of minced garlic

METHOD

1. Mix all marinade ingredients together and pour into marinade container.

2. Place beef cubes into marinade for approximately 1 hour for a lot of flavour or about half an hour for a more subtle taste. This marinade is very rich so if you don't like a very strong taste only glaze the kebabs.

3. Place kebab sticks in a large container and add one tablespoon of oil. This makes it easier to thread beef and vegetables.

4. Thread beef and chopped vegies onto kebab sticks and barbecue.

Thanks to Melissa Rayner, Ararat, VIC.

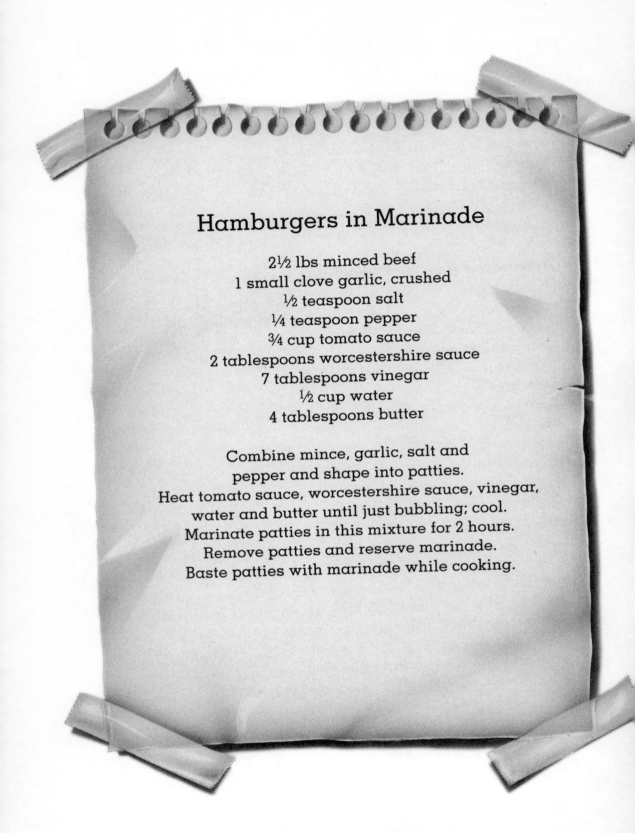

Hamburgers in Marinade

2½ lbs minced beef
1 small clove garlic, crushed
½ teaspoon salt
¼ teaspoon pepper
¾ cup tomato sauce
2 tablespoons worcestershire sauce
7 tablespoons vinegar
½ cup water
4 tablespoons butter

Combine mince, garlic, salt and
pepper and shape into patties.
Heat tomato sauce, worcestershire sauce, vinegar,
water and butter until just bubbling; cool.
Marinate patties in this mixture for 2 hours.
Remove patties and reserve marinade.
Baste patties with marinade while cooking.

This recipe courtesy of Shirley Clampit, Port Lincoln, SA.

Steaks with a Red Wine and Blue Cheese Topping

Serves 4

125 g creamy blue cheese
2 tablespoons red wine
1 teaspoon French mustard
1 teaspoon snipped fresh chives
1 clove garlic, crushed
4 sirloin steaks
2 tablespoons oil
salt and pepper to taste

1. Combine cheese, wine, mustard, chives and garlic.
2. Brush steaks with 1 tablespoon oil. Season to taste with salt and pepper. Cook steak on one side over high heat for 2–3 minutes or until juices start appearing on the uncooked side. If you like your steak rare, turn over, top with cheese mixture, and continue cooking for a further 2–3 minutes. If you like your steak medium or well done, seal on both sides for 2–3 minutes, move to a cooler part of the barbecue and continue cooking for a further 2–3 minutes each side for medium and 4–6 minutes each side for well done. Add topping when turning for the last time.
3. Serve in a toasted roll with tomato, lettuce and cucumber.

Beef a la Clarence
Serves 4

1 ripe avocado
12 green king prawns
4 rib fillet steaks

Béarnaise Sauce
1/3 cup white vinegar
3 black peppercorns
2 teaspoons fresh tarragon
2 shallots
2 egg yolks
125 g butter

I tried this Tracey it was very very good — thanks K.

Split avocado in half lengthways and remove seed and skin.
Slice avocado lengthways and set aside.

Shell prawns leaving tails intact, remove veins.
Cook steaks on hot greased barbecue plate until tender.
Barbecue prawns just before removing the steak.
Place 1/4 of avocado and three king prawns on top of each steak.
Cover prawns with béarnaise sauce.
Serve with a crisp green salad.

For Béarnaise sauce: Combine vinegar, peppercorns, chopped tarragon and shallots in pan. Bring to boil, simmer uncovered until reduced by half. Strain mixture.

Blend eggs in food processor. Add vinegar liquid and blend until smooth.

Melt butter in microwave until hot and bubbling. Gradually pour in hot butter while blender is running. Blend until thick and smooth.

This recipe is from Tracey Graham, Chef, Bridge Restaurant, Key Lodge Motel, Grafton, NSW.

Steak with Lemon Anchovy Butter

Serves 4

125 g butter, softened
4 anchovy fillets, mashed
1/4 cup finely chopped fresh parsley
1 clove garlic, crushed
1 teaspoon grated lemon rind
1 teaspoon French mustard
1 teaspoon white wine vinegar
4 t-bone steaks
1 tablespoon oil
salt and pepper to taste

1. Place the butter in a bowl and add the anchovies, parsley, garlic, lemon rind, mustard and vinegar. Mix well to combine. Spoon onto a piece of foil and roll up into a log shape. Refrigerate until ready to use.
2. Brush steaks with oil and season to taste with salt and pepper. Barbecue over high heat for 2–3 minutes each side. If you like your steak rare, remove straight away. If you like your meat medium or well done, move the steaks to a cooler part of the barbecue and continue cooking for a further 2–3 minutes each side for medium and 4–6 minutes each side for well done.
3. Remove anchovy butter from refrigerator and slice into rounds. Serve steak topped with a pat of anchovy butter, accompanied by potato salad and coleslaw.

Dear Mr. Laws,

I would like you to use this good recipe from Kununurra. We all grew up on it and even now I cook it for my family.

Good Kimberley Jerky

Cut your beef into thin strips, put it all into a bowl and marinate in soy sauce, Mexican chilli powder, brown sugar, coriander and any other spice or herb you might like. Put it into the fridge for about two or three days stirring at least once a day. When the beef is completely saturated with the marinade, thread onto skewers and hang out to dry, high enough over the top of your BBQ so it dries and smokes but, doesn't cook.

Make sure the dogs can't get near it because they'll steal it. When it's dry you put it in a jar but mostly it's all gone before then. It's also very good for teething rusks — the little kids love it.

From Nowela Mirrawung, Wherrol Flat, NSW.

VEAL

Veal Shoulder Stuffed with Prosciutto, Capers and Lemon

Serves 4

1 boned shoulder of veal
$1/4$ cup fresh breadcrumbs
1 slice prosciutto (or rindless bacon rashers), chopped
1 shallots, finely chopped
2 teaspoons capers
grated rind $1/4$ lemon
1 tablespoon lemon juice
1 tablespoon chopped blanched almonds
1 tablespoon chopped fresh parsley
2 teaspoons chopped fresh basil
salt and pepper to taste
1 tablespoon oil

1. Weigh veal to calculate cooking time, allowing 45 minutes per 500g. Lay the veal out and cut through the thickest part of the meat to open it out.
2. Combine the breadcrumbs, prosciutto, shallots, capers, lemon rind and juice, almonds, parsley and basil in a bowl. Season to taste with salt and pepper. Spread over veal.
3. Roll veal up and tie securely with string. Brush with oil and barbecue over medium heat for calculated cooking time or until cooked through. Allow to stand for 10-15 minutes before carving.
4. Serve with jacket potatoes and salad.

Veal Stuffed with Swiss Cheese and Rosemary

Serves 4

4 veal chops, cut about 2.5 cm thick
4 slices Swiss cheese, cut into strips
4 slices ham, cut into strips
1 teaspoon dried rosemary
cracked black pepper
1 tablespoon oil

1. Cut a pocket horizontally in each of the chops. Combine the cheese, ham and rosemary in a bowl. Season to taste with cracked black pepper. Fill pockets with cheese mixture. Close openings with toothpicks.
2. Brush chops with oil and barbecue for 7-10 minutes each side or until cooked through.
3. Serve with a simple cheesy risotto and green salad.

See picture on page 38.

Veal Rolls with Ham and Sage

Serve 4

4 veal schnitzels
1 tablespoon French mustard
4 slices ham
4 slices Swiss cheese
4 button mushrooms, sliced
4 tablespoons fresh breadcrumbs
4 fresh sage leaves
1 tablespoon oil
salt and pepper to taste

1. Lay out each schnitzel on a flat surface. Spread each one with 1 teaspoon mustard. Top with a slice of ham and cheese and mushroom slices. Sprinkle with breadcrumbs and lay a sage leaf on each one. Fold sides in and roll up to form a neat parcel. Tie securely with string.
2. Brush rolls with oil and season to taste with salt and pepper. Barbecue over medium heat for 4-5 minutes each side.
3. Serve veal rolls with a green salad and a medley of cooked diced carrots, peas and corn in a mayonnaise dressing.

See picture on page 38.

Veal Chops with Basil and Lemon

Serves 4

4 veal chops
$1/2$ cup olive oil
2 tablespoons lemon juice
2 tablespoons chopped fresh basil
$1/2$ teaspoon dried lemon thyme
salt and pepper to taste

1. Place the veal chops in a shallow dish. Combine the oil, lemon juice, basil and lemon thyme in a bowl. Season to taste with salt and pepper. Pour over veal and turn chops to coat both sides. Cover and refrigerate for at least 4 hours or overnight.
2. Drain chops and reserve marinade. Barbecue over medium heat for 7-10 minutes each side or until cooked through, basting with marinade from time to time.
3. Serve with a potato salad, perhaps with some fennel added.

See picture on page 38.

LAMB

Creamy Lamb with Lemongrass

Serves 4

15 g butter
2 stalks lemongrass
2 tablespoons grated fresh ginger
1 small red chilli, seeded and chopped
1 cup coconut cream
4 lamb leg steaks

1. Heat the butter in a small saucepan and saute the lemongrass, ginger and chilli for 2 minutes, stirring occasionally. Remove from heat and stir in the coconut cream.
2. Place the lamb leg steaks in a shallow dish. Pour coconut mixture over lamb, cover and refrigerate for 2 hours.
3. Drain lamb and reserve marinade. Barbecue lamb over medium/high heat for 4-6 minutes each side, or until cooked to taste.
4. Meanwhile, place the marinade into a small saucepan and simmer gently for 2-3 minutes. Do not let mixture boil hard or sauce may curdle.
5. Serve with steamed rice and stir-fried baby bok choy.

Right: Lamb Kebabs with Indian Spices (top left), recipe page 59;
Creamy Lamb with Lemongrass (top right);
Lamb with Apricot and Mint Seasoning (front), recipe page 61

Lamburgers in Pitta Bread

Serves 4

2 slices bread, crusts removed
$1/4$ cup milk
500 g lamb mince
$1/4$ cup finely chopped fresh parsley
$1/4$ cup pine nuts, toasted and chopped
$1/2$ teaspoon mixed spice
$1/4$ teaspoon ground cinnamon
salt and pepper to taste
8 pitta pockets
200 g tub hummos
4 tomatoes, chopped
200 g sour cream
shredded lettuce

1. Soak the bread in the milk for 10 minutes, then mash well. Place into a bowl with the mince, parsley, pine nuts, mixed spice, cinnamon, salt and pepper. Mix well to combine.
2. With wet hands, form mince mixture into 8 patties about 1cm thick. Cover and refrigerate for 30 minutes.
3. Cook burgers on a lightly oiled hot plate for about 3 minutes each side or until cooked to taste.
4. Slice open one side of each pitta pocket, spread with hummos and fill with lamburgers, tomatoes, sour cream and lettuce.

Left: Lamburgers in Pitta Bread (right); Lamb Shanks with Wine and Lemon Marinade (front), recipe page 63; Lamb Loin with Spicy Almond Seasoning (left), recipe page 65

Devilled Lamb Spareribs

2½ cups lemon juice
8 cloves of garlic, sliced
4 tsp each salt, dry mustard and chilli powder
2 tsp ground cumin
1 tbs thyme leaves
½ tsp pepper
10 lamb spareribs
paprika

Combine lemon juice, garlic, salt, mustard, chilli powder, cumin, thyme and pepper. Pour over lamb in large shallow dish or pan.

Marinate several hours or overnight.

Place spareribs on rack in shallow roasting pan; reserve marinade.

Roast lamb 1 hour and 30 minutes, basting occasionally with marinade. Sprinkle with paprika; roast 30 minutes longer or until tender. Garnish with thickly sliced tomatoes and parsley.

Recipe supplied by Dee Hoffman, The Gap, QLD.

Lamb Kebabs with Indian Spices

Serves 4

750 g diced lamb
1 onion, finely chopped
2 cloves garlic, crushed
2 red chillies, seeded and chopped (or to taste)
2 tablespoons lemon juice
2 teaspoons grated fresh ginger
2 teaspoons garam masala
2 teaspoons ground coriander
2 teaspoons ground cumin
2 teaspoons ground cinnamon
1 teaspoon ground cardamom
freshly grated nutmeg to taste
2 whole cloves
salt and pepper to taste
200 g natural yoghurt
bamboo skewers, soaked in water for 30 minutes

1. Place the lamb in a bowl. Combine the onion, garlic, chillies, lemon juice, ginger, garam masala, coriander, cumin, cinnamon, cardamom, nutmeg and cloves in a bowl. Season to taste with salt and pepper. Stir in the yoghurt and mix well to combine. Pour over lamb and stir to coat meat well. Cover and refrigerate for 8 hours or overnight.
2. Thread lamb pieces onto skewers and barbecue over high heat for 8–10 minutes or until cooked to taste.
3. Serve lamb with rice, pappadums and side dishes of banana and coconut, tomato and onion, and cucumber and yoghurt, if desired.

See picture on page 55.

One of Kerida's restaurants in Australia

Mask Of China
RESTAURANT

Char-grilled Lamb Cutlets

Ingredients
12 French lamb cutlets
1 tablespoon Chinese rosedew wine or sweet sherry
1 tablespoon plum sauce
3 tablespoons hoisin sauce
4 tablespoons sugar
1 tablespoon salt
¼ teaspoon Chinese five spice powder
honey, to glaze
water, to glaze

Method
Place lamb cutlets in a large bowl. Mix all other ingredients well and pour over lamb cutlets. Cover and leave to marinate for 3–4 hours. Cook lamb over char-griller turning several times. Before serving, glaze with a mixture of honey and water.

This recipe is from Mask of China Restaurant, Melbourne, VIC.

Lamb with Apricot and Mint Seasoning

Serves 4–6

1 shoulder of lamb, boned
$^1/_2$ cup fresh breadcrumbs
$^1/_4$ cup chopped dried apricots
$^1/_4$ cup chopped fresh mint
$^1/_4$ cup chopped fresh parsley
1 slice ham, finely chopped
1 clove garlic, crushed
1 tablespoon pine nuts, toasted
1 tablespoon lemon juice
salt and pepper to taste
1 tablespoon oil
60 g butter, softened
1 tablespoon German mustard

1. Weigh the lamb to calculate the cooking time, allowing 25–30 minutes per 500 g. Lay shoulder out on a flat surface, skin-side down. Trim away any fat.
2. Place breadcrumbs in a bowl with the apricots, mint, parsley, ham, garlic, pine nuts and lemon juice. Season to taste with salt and pepper. Spread mixture over lamb, roll up and secure tightly with string. Cover and refrigerate for 8 hours or overnight.
3. Brush lamb with oil and season to taste with salt and pepper. Barbecue over medium heat for calculated cooking time or until cooked to taste. During the last 20 minutes of cooking, baste lamb with combined butter and mustard every 5 minutes. Allow to stand for 10–15 minutes before carving.
4. Serve with char-grilled vegetables, such as eggplant and capsicum.

See picture on page 55.

Dear John,

I've just taken one week's annual leave to build a covered barbecue area over our patio. Unfortunately my job does not allow me to listen to your show. But while I was working on our patio I was listening to your show and heard about the barbecue book competition.

As I love cooking barbecues, I thought I would send you one of our favourite recipes. I hope it is worthy of a place in your book, but if not I hope you try it yourself.

I know there will be some wonderful recipes in the book, so if you would kindly record my name and address, on completion of the book contact me and I will forward the appropriate amount.

Thank you

P. S. My given name is Geoffrey but my great aunt and grandmother were the only ones to call me Geoffrey, to everyone else I'm Pud.

Lamb Chops with Vermouth

8 lamb chops

Marinade
1 cup dry vermouth
1 cup salad oil
1 tablespoon lemon juice
1 onion, chopped
2 teaspoons minced garlic
1 teaspoon dried tarragon
1 teaspoon dried basil
1 teaspoon salt
approx ½–1 teaspoon ground pepper

Mix all marinade ingredients together. Put chops in marinade dish or baking dish. Pour marinade over, cover and leave for at least 4 hrs, turning often. Barbecue over hot grill until cooked to taste, basting with marinade during cooking.

Thanks to Pud Jenkins from Geraldton, WA.

Lamb Shanks with Wine and Lemon Marinade

Serves 4

4 large lamb shanks
2 cloves garlic, sliced
1 cup white wine
$1/4$ cup olive oil
grated rind and juice 1 lemon
1 red chilli, seeded and chopped
2 tablespoons chopped fresh mint
salt and pepper to taste

1. With a sharp knife, make small incisions in the lamb shanks. Push a slice of garlic into each cut. Place in a shallow dish.
2. Combine the wine, oil, lemon rind and juice, chilli and mint in a bowl. Season to taste with salt and pepper. Pour over shanks and turn to coat well in marinade. Cover and refrigerate for 8 hours or overnight.
3. Drain shanks and reserve marinade. Brown shanks over high heat on the barbecue, then move to medium/low heat, baste with the marinade, and continue cooking for a further $1-1^1/2$ hours or until cooked to taste, basting with marinade every 15 minutes.
4. Serve with sauteed potatoes and sugar snap peas.

See picture on page 56.

RESTAURANT

Gippsland Baby Lamb Rump Marinated with Honey and Olive Oil with Jerusalem Artichoke Parcels and Spiced Mint Sauce

Serves 4

4 baby lamb rumps — score top layer with a sharp knife
4 rosemary spikes with some leaves attached — push through centre
of rump as a skewer

Make a marinade of 3 tblspns of honey and 2 tblspns of olive oil and
cracked black pepper. Add lamb then marinate for approx. 20 hours
turning frequently. When ready to barbecue, seal both sides on high
heat then continue cooking on low heat for 15 minutes for medium rare.

Jerusalem Artichoke Parcels
12 Jerusalem artichokes, peeled
8 French shallots, peeled
8 garlic cloves, peeled but left whole
4 tspns butter
salt and pepper

Make 4 separate airtight foil parcels containing equal amounts of these
ingredients and using double thickness of foil. To cook, place on side of
barbecue where it is not too hot and bake for approx. 20 minutes. Rotate
occasionally to ensure even cooking.

Mint Sauce
Simmer 200 gm sugar and 100 ml of water until liquid starts to
change colour. Add a touch of freshly chopped chilli, some grated ginger, a
good dash of balsamic vinegar and some finely chopped fresh mint.
Remove from heat and serve hot or cold with lamb.

Bon Appetit
Niklas Eberhardt, Head Chef

If you go to La grilladé send Jennie my love — yes Jennie!

This recipe is from La Grillade Restaurant, Crows Nest, NSW.

Lamb Loin with Spicy Almond Seasoning

Serves 4

1 kg boned lamb loin
2 cloves garlic, sliced
75 g blanched almonds, toasted
$1/2$ cup fresh breadcrumbs
60 g butter, melted
1 teaspoon chilli powder
1 teaspoon dried oregano
$1/4$ teaspoon ground cloves
$1/4$ teaspoon ground coriander
$1/4$ teaspoon ground cinnamon
2 tomatoes, peeled, seeded and finely chopped
salt and pepper to taste
1 tablespoon oil

1. Trim lamb of any fat and make small incisions in the meat with a sharp knife. Push garlic slices into cuts.
2. Place the almonds in a food processor and process until chopped. Place in a bowl with the breadcrumbs, butter, chilli powder, oregano, cloves, coriander, cinnamon, tomatoes and salt and pepper to taste. Mix well. Spread seasoning onto lamb and roll up, tying securely with string. Cover and refrigerate for 2 hours.
3. Brush lamb with oil and season with salt and pepper. Barbecue over medium heat for 50–60 minutes or until cooked to taste. Allow to rest for 10–15 minutes before carving.
4. Serve with rice and a salad, perhaps using spinach leaves.

See picture on page 56.

Grilled Mandalong Lamb Loin with Onion Marmalade and Charred New Potatoes

Onion Marmalade

250 gm Spanish onions
1 tbs olive oil
30 gm sugar
80 ml white wine vinegar
1 clove
½ bay leaf
¼ tsp ground black pepper
¼ tsp salt
½ tbs tomato paste
½ tbs cayenne pepper

Method
1. Sauté finely diced onion in olive oil until transparent. Add all other ingredients except cayenne pepper and cook gently for 2 hours, stir occasionally.
2. Add cayenne pepper and cool.
3. Serve chilled.

Mandalong Lamb Loin

1 kg Mandalong lamb loin
1 tbs olive oil
1 tsp crushed black pepper
½ tsp sweet paprika
pinch nutmeg
rock salt
new potatoes, baby carrots, navets, baby squash, spring onions, snow peas, fresh Greek basil, to serve

Method
1. Baste loin with olive oil and rub in seasoning except the salt.
2. Char-grill from all sides to your liking (medium-done lamb is the best as it brings out the best flavours).
3. Slice potatoes and boil until tender (not too soft).
4. Char-grill potatoes on both sides.
5. Boil baby vegetables and toss with butter and finely chopped Greek basil.
6. Once lamb is cooked, season outside with rock salt.
7. Slice lamb loin into wedges, sprinkle onion marmalade around plate and serve with char-grilled new potatoes and baby vegetables.

This recipe is from Siggi's at The Heritage Restaurant, Brisbane, QLD.

Lamb with Spinach and Almond Stuffing

Serves 4-6

1 tablespoon olive oil
1 medium onion, chopped
2 cups chopped fresh spinach
1^1/2 cups fresh breadcrumbs
^{1}/2 cup flaked almonds, toasted
1 egg, lightly beaten
1 teaspoon dried rosemary leaves
1 butterflied leg of lamb
^{1}/4 cup marmalade
1 tablespoon butter, softened
1 teaspoon dried rosemary leaves, extra

1. Prepare an indirect fire in the kettle barbecue. Allow to heat for at least 1 hour with the lid off.
2. Meanwhile, to make stuffing, heat oil in a frypan. Fry onion until tender. Add spinach, cook until soft. Combine onion and spinach with breadcrumbs, almonds, egg and rosemary. Spread mixture over inside of lamb. Roll up and tie with wet string to keep lamb in shape while it cooks. Weigh lamb to calculate the cooking time.
3. Combine marmalade, butter and extra rosemary. Spread mixture over the surface of the lamb. Place lamb in kettle barbecue. Cover and roast with vent open. Per 500 g, allow 20-25 minutes for rare, 25-30 minutes for medium, or 30-35 minutes for well done. The total cooking time will be about 1^1/2 hours. Brush occasionally with meat cooking juices.
4. When cooked, remove lamb from barbecue. Leave to rest for 20 minutes in a warm place, covered loosely with foil, before carving.
5. Serve with char-grilled vegetables and a salad.

Cook's tip: This recipe is also suitable for oven roasting at 180°C. Use orange, lemon or lime marmalade for the baste. Pine nuts can be used in the stuffing in place of almonds.

Chilli Lamb Satays

Serves 4-6

1 medium onion, roughly chopped
2 cloves garlic, peeled
1-2 medium red chillies, seeds removed
2 tablespoons desiccated coconut
3 tablespoons lemon juice
2 tablespoons soy sauce
750 g diced Trim Lamb (prepared from round or topside)
$1/2$ cup peanut butter (smooth or crunchy)
$1/2$ cup hot water
few drops chilli sauce (optional)
12-18 pappadums

1. Place onion, garlic, chillies, coconut, 2 tablespoons of the juice and 1 tablespoon of soy sauce in a food processor; process to a thickish paste. Place meat in a large dish and stir the onion mixture through; leave to marinate in a cool place for 10 minutes.
2. Preheat barbecue on high. Thread the lamb on oiled skewers. Barbecue for 8-10 minutes, turning occasionally.
3. Place peanut butter, water and chilli sauce in a small pan and stir over medium heat until smooth. Remove from heat, stir in remaining juice and soy sauce.
4. Cook pappadums, six at a time, in a microwave oven on High (100% power) for 1 minute. (Do not use a convection-type microwave oven because arcing may occur.) Serve with kebabs and sauce.

Middle Eastern Style BBQ Lamb

400 grams of deboned loin of lamb
  (or lamb back-straps)
1 tbsp olive oil
2 tsp cumin powder
1 clove garlic, chopped
1 tbsp ground coriander
1/2 tsp paprika
pinch of cinnamon
little lemon juice
1/2 tsp of chilli paste (optional)
little freshly ground black pepper

Cut the loin in 3-4 cm slices. (If you get the lamb back-straps, there is no need for cutting. You can also ask your butcher to do this for you.)

Mix olive oil, cumin, garlic, coriander, cinnamon, paprika, lemon juice, chilli paste and little black pepper.

Toss the lamb in this marinade and allow to stand for about 2 hours.

Cook the lamb on a hot clean barbecue for about 3 minutes on each side depending how you like your meat done.

Serve with couscous and chick peas.

Elly Overeem provided this recipe.

Barbecued Lamb Ribs with Capsicum Salsa

Serves 4

2 sets of lamb party ribs
1/4–1/3 cup prepared teriyaki sauce
Salsa
2 tablespoons sunflower oil
1 medium onion, quartered
1 medium red capsicum, coarsely chopped
1 teaspoon freshly crushed garlic
410 g can peeled tomatoes, roughly chopped
1 tablespoon balsamic vinegar
1 tablespoon maple syrup
1/4 teaspoon cracked black peppercorns
1/4 teaspoon minced chillies

1. Marinate ribs in teriyaki sauce for at least 1 hour, or overnight if you have the time.
2. To make the salsa, heat oil in a frying pan on high. Fry the onion and capsicum 5 minutes. Add garlic, tomatoes with their liquid, vinegar, maple syrup, pepper and chilli. Simmer, uncovered, 15 minutes or until mixture is slightly thickened.
3. Heat barbecue on high. (For wood or charcoal barbecues, heat to glowing coals — no flames.)
4. Drain ribs, reserving marinade as a baste. Cook ribs until well browned and sealed, 7–8 minutes each side, basting occasionally with the marinade.
Serving tip: To serve as finger food, slice the ribs and serve the salsa as a dipping sauce.

Cook's tips: This recipe is also suitable for grilling or for roasting in the oven.
Always wash your hands after handling chillies and chilli spice. The 'heat' of the chillies can irritate and 'burn' your skin. Be sure not to touch your eyes.

JUMBUCK MUTTON SHANKS

Buy whole sheep shank bones, (not cut) one or two for each person.

I suggest 1 per adult, off leg & 1 per child, off shoulder.

Slice through sinews at the bottom end of the knuckle & push the meat down towards the larger mass of meat.

Place in a boiler & just cover with water.

Add a few bay leaves, cloves, peppercorns & a desertspoon of cider vinegar. Add pinch salt, bring to the boil & simmer until tender.

Take off heat to one side & leave in water to cool & then drain.

Note: If you take the fat that has set off the top of this liquid it makes a good soup base.

THE SEEP: In a bowl pour ½ cup of Olive oil, ¾ cup cider vinegar, (1 tablespoon of tomato & pick-me-up sauce here is optional)?, sweeten to taste with 7 to 9 teaspoons of sugar & about a cup of finely chopped Mint leaves, black pepper to taste & mix thoroughly.

Place shanks in a dish & pour Seep mixture over & around them & leave for the day, turning them every now & then.

Remove from Seep to cook on the hot plate tossing around until heated well right through. Best done on "Fair Dinkum 44".

TO SERVE: Double bands of Alfoil and wrap around the meatless end of the bone area. (This is for holding & chewing the bone). Serve with Potatoes coated in Olive oil and sprinkled with sesame seeds.

Follow with Damper spread with Cockies Joy & Billy Tea.

These Barbecued Jumbuck Shanks are sumptuous, for taste and cost they are unrivalled, saving you £'s, while being ritzy.

Lorna A. Warwick. L.A.W.
26/03/1996   INVERELL.

If using a shovel for grill, position yourself on the downside of the wind as it is sure to change suddenly.

PORK

Barbecued Pork Chops

Serves 4

4 pork loin chops
2 tablespoons oil
salt and pepper to taste

1. If pork has a rind, cut through it at 2 cm intervals to stop meat curling while cooking. Brush chops with oil and season to taste with salt and pepper.
2. Set a gas or electric barbecue to medium heat. If using charcoal or wood, build a good fire, then let it die down until the coals turn white.
3. Cook chops on one side for 7–10 minutes or until juices appear on the uncooked side. Turn over and cook for a further 7–10 minutes or until cooked through.

Right: Barbecued Pork and Prunes (top), recipe page 75; Ham Steaks with an Orange Whisky Sauce (middle), recipe page 76; Pork and Apple Focaccia (front), recipe page 78

Barbecued Pork and Prunes

Some cuts of pork I just can't take to — I am not a lover of pork — I sometimes find it too fatty. But if you find a good cut, like the shoulder, you can do wonderful things with little cubes of pork and a packet of prunes, believe it or not.

Ingredients

let's say about 500 g boneless pork shoulder cut into cubes, about 2 cm each.
1 packet of prunes — stoned prunes.
   No! Not you — the prunes.
2 tablespoons olive oil
2 teaspoons lemon juice
lemon rind, grated

Mix the pork and the prunes together. Mix the oil, lemon juice and rind then roll the pork and prunes in and let them stand for 10 minutes or so. Thread the pork and prunes alternately onto the skewers and put them close to the coals to seal the meat on all sides. Then raise the skewers away from the heat — about 10–12 cm above the coals — and cook for 15 minutes, turning the skewers all the time.

Left: Hot and Spicy Pork Chops (left), recipe page 82; Chinese-Style Spare Ribs (front), recipe page 80

Ham Steaks with an Orange Whisky Sauce

Serves 4

$1/4$ cup orange juice concentrate
1 tablespoon Worcestershire sauce
1 tablespoon oil
salt and pepper to taste
4 ham steaks, about 1 cm thick
1 tablespoon cornflour
1 cup water
$1/2$ cup chunky orange marmalade
2 tablespoons whisky

1. Combine the orange juice concentrate, Worcestershire sauce and oil in a bowl. Season to taste with salt and pepper.
2. Place ham in a shallow dish, pour marinade over and turn steaks to coat well. Cover and refrigerate for 2 hours.
3. Drain ham and reserve marinade. Barbecue ham over medium heat for 3-4 minutes each side or until cooked to taste.
4. Meanwhile, place the marinade in a saucepan. Blend the cornflour with a little of the water to form a smooth paste. Add to the marinade with the remaining water, marmalade and whisky. Bring to the boil, reduce heat and simmer until thickened.
5. Serve ham with the sauce, accompanied by a Waldorf salad.

Maiale alla Salvia e Castagne
Pork chops with sage and chestnuts

Ingredients
(for 6 people)
20 medium-sized chestnuts
6 large pork chops
300 ml olive oil
30 sage leaves
4 cloves garlic
Salt and pepper
50 ml wine vinegar

Nobody can make it like Beppi but its worth a Try
B.

Directions
Boil chestnuts in salted water, approximately 5 minutes, then peel.

Beat the pork chops, leaving some fat around the edges. Marinate in olive oil, sage, garlic, and salt and pepper for 1 hour. Place on the barbecue and cook through.

In a pan over a strong fire place chestnuts and vinegar, cover with a lid. Cook on medium heat for 10 minutes or until sauce is reduced. Add salt and freshly ground pepper.

Pour sauce with the chestnuts over the chops and garnish with sage leaves and garlic.

Serve with mashed potatoes and pan-sautéed English spinach, cooked with 2 cloves of garlic.

This recipe courtesy of Beppi Polese, Proprietor, Ristorante Beppis, East Sydney, NSW.

Pork and Apple Focaccia

Serves 4

4 pork leg steaks
1/4 cup olive oil
1 tablespoon lemon juice
2 bay leaves
1 teaspoon chopped fresh sage
salt and pepper to taste
4 red Delicious apples, cored and cut into 1 cm thick slices
1 tablespoon lemon juice, extra
2 tablespoons soft brown sugar
1/2 cup green tomato chutney
4 pieces focaccia, toasted

1. Place the pork leg steaks into a shallow dish. Pour over combined oil, lemon juice, bay leaves, sage and salt and pepper. Cover and refrigerate for at least 4 hours, or overnight.
2. Drain pork and reserve marinade. Barbecue over medium heat for 7–10 minutes each side or until cooked through, brushing with marinade while cooking.
3. As the steaks are cooking, brush the apple slices with the extra lemon juice and cook alongside the steak for 3 minutes. Turn apples over and sprinkle with brown sugar. Continue cooking until apples are tender but still hold their shape.
4. Slice pork and serve with the apple slices and green tomato chutney in the toasted focaccia.

See picture on page 73.

Tropical Pork Kebabs BBQ

Ingredients:

150g Pork Mince
4 bacon rashers
1 cup fresh breadcrumbs
1 tblspn fresh parsley chopped
1 onion grated
Black pepper
Cubes of fruit - pineapple / melon / apple /
kiwi fruit (according to season)

Method:

Combine pork mince, finely chopped bacon rashers, breadcrumbs, parsley, onion and pepper.

Mould into egg shapes and place one onto end of each skewer.

BBQ for 15-20 minutes turning 2-3 times. When cooked thread fresh fruit onto the other end of skewer.

Enjoy!

Thanks to Mrs Heather Cowen, Yeronga, QLD, for this recipe.

Chinese-Style Spare Ribs

Serves 4

1 kg pork rack ribs
4 shallots, finely chopped
1 clove garlic, chopped
$1/4$ cup soy sauce
1 tablespoon sesame oil
1 tablespoon honey
1 tablespoon hoisin sauce
1 tablespoon dry sherry
2 teaspoons lemon juice
2 teaspoons five spice powder
$1/4$ cup plum jam

1. Place the ribs in a shallow dish. Combine the shallots, garlic, soy sauce, sesame oil, honey, hoisin sauce, sherry, lemon juice and five spice powder in a bowl. Pour over ribs, turning to coat well. Cover and refrigerate overnight.
2. Drain ribs and barbecue over medium/low heat for 45–60 minutes or until almost cooked.
3. Heat the plum jam in a small saucepan until melted. Brush ribs with jam every 5 minutes for a further 15 minutes.
4. Serve with rice and stir-fried vegetables, such as snow peas, baby corn, capsicum and bean sprouts.

See picture on page 74.

Verna's Pork Spareribs

1 kg pork spareribs
salt
brown sugar

Marinade
4 tablespoons soy sauce
2 tablespoons dry sherry
2 tablespoons oil
2 tablespoons brown sugar
2–4 cloves garlic, crushed
1 teaspoon ground ginger
2 tablespoons sesame seeds
2 tablespoons finely chopped spring onions or chives

Trim fat from the ribs and slash pieces of rib every 2 cm with a sharp knife. Sprinkle with salt and rub a little brown sugar into the bone.

Make the marinade, add ribs and leave to steep for at least 2 hours — longer for a more pronounced flavour.

Grill over slow coals.

Verna Pearce of Narrikup, WA, provided this recipe.

Hot and Spicy Pork Chops

Serves 4

4 pork loin chops
$1/4$ cup orange juice concentrate
$1/4$ cup dry white wine
1 tablespoon honey
1 tablespoon curry powder (or to taste)
1 teaspoon grated fresh ginger
$1/2$ teaspoon garam masala

1. If the chops have a rind, cut it at 2 cm intervals to stop meat curling while cooking. Place chops in a shallow dish. Combine the orange juice concentrate, wine, honey, curry powder, ginger and garam masala in a bowl. Mix well. Pour over chops, and turn to coat well. Cover and refrigerate for 2 hours.
2. Drain chops and reserve marinade. Barbecue chops over medium heat for 7–10 minutes each side or until cooked through, turning and basting with marinade while cooking.
3. Serve with steamed rice and side dishes of banana and coconut, tomato and onion, and cucumber and yoghurt.

See picture on page 74.

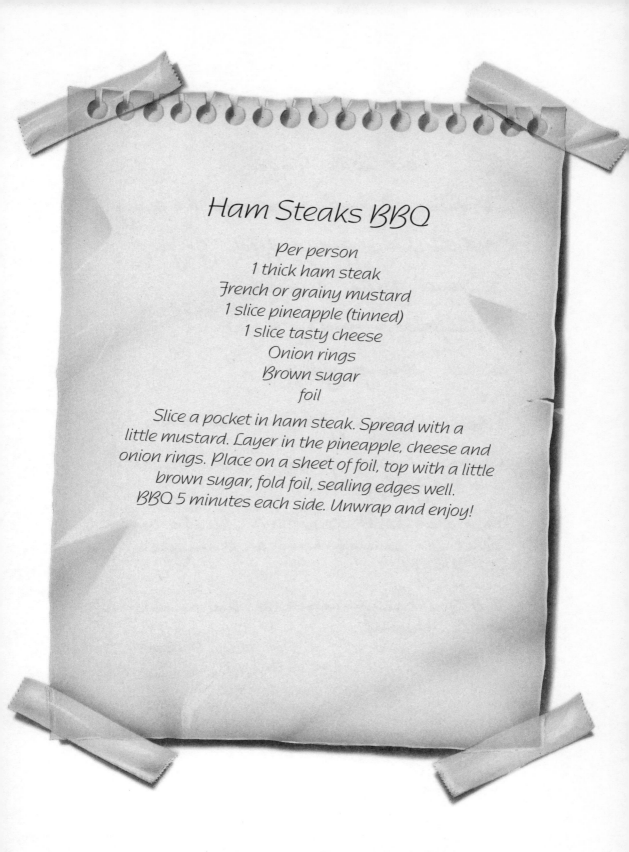

Ham Steaks BBQ

Per person
1 thick ham steak
French or grainy mustard
1 slice pineapple (tinned)
1 slice tasty cheese
Onion rings
Brown sugar
foil

Slice a pocket in ham steak. Spread with a little mustard. Layer in the pineapple, cheese and onion rings. Place on a sheet of foil, top with a little brown sugar, fold foil, sealing edges well. BBQ 5 minutes each side. Unwrap and enjoy!

Recipe from Mrs Marie Ahsee, Toowoomba, QLD.

Pork with Ginger

6 pieces of pork suitable for B.B.Queing

3 tablespoons grated fresh ginger

3 cloves garlic crushed

2 tablespoons brown sugar

¾ cup orange juice

Place pork in glass casserole dish

Combine ginger, garlic, brown sugar and orange juice

Pour over pork, cover with plastic wrap, leave for several hours or overnight in fridge

B.B.Q, pouring marinade over meat while cooking

Judy Packer
Logan Reserve Qld

Thanks to Judy Packer, Logan Reserve, QLD.

Sisco's Restaurant

121 MACQUARIE STREET, HOBART, TASMANIA   PHONE: 23 2059

Thankyou for giving me the opportunity to submit a suggestion for your book. This typically Catalan recipe will adapt beautifully to a balmy Aussie evening, to be enjoyed with wine and good company. Some pre-cooking preparation is required but is well worth the effort. I hope you will enjoy it as much as I have.

Llom de Porc amb Escalivada

(Marinated pork loin with char-grilled vegetables)
Serves 4

For the Pork Loin
1 kg pork loin, boned and skinned
5 tblspns paprika
3 tspns oregano
1 tspn freshly ground black peppercorns
6 cloves garlic, finely minced
2 tspns salt
1 cup olive oil
1/2 cup water

To begin, we shall combine all the above ingredients except for the pork. Blend well until a deep red runny paste is achieved. Then immerse the pork loin into it ensuring that all sides of the loin have come into contact with the mix. Let the marinated pork loin rest in a cool place for at least 24 hours.

For the Char-grilled Vegetables
2 red capsicum
2 green capsicum
2 scallions
1 eggplant
olive oil

Escalivar is the Catalan word for cooking over hot embers. Escalivada is the equivalent using char-grilled vegetables, rubbed with oil and cooked whole. In the summertime we frequently used it to accompany a variety of courses. If a char-griller is used, the escalivada will develop a mouth-watering smoky flavour.

Let's rub all the vegetables with liberal amounts of olive oil. Place them on the hot coals or char-grill and let the skin of the vegetables toast and roast until it virtually starts to crack off. Care must be taken not to burn the vegetables beyond their protective skin, but at the same time they need to be cooked all the way through, especially the eggplant. Rotate them frequently.

Peel the eggplant and capsicums. With your fingers tear them into very thin strips. Arrange them on a platter and season with salt and pepper, drizzle with more olive oil. Serve at room temperature with the pork.

When one is ready to cook the pork, cut thin 5 mm—8 mm slices of the loin (4—5 slices per person), re-dip them in the marinade and char-grill, leaving neat bar marks on each side. Take care not to overcook.

Serve the pork with the escalivada, a bowl of olives and a fresh crisp salad sprinkled with lemon juice and garlic. A glass of red and crusty bread. I guarantee it will be a delightful evening. Enjoy.

This recipe is from Seb Bosch, Sisco's Restaurant, Hobart, TAS.

John,

I have road tested (so to speak) this dish on friends and relatives with great success. It can be used as an appetizer or with a main meal.

Love your show keep up the good work.

Pig on the Cob

A real quick and easy appetizer guaranteed to get those taste buds going. Warning: Do not make too many, otherwise they will not eat the steaks.

To make about 20, you will need:

1 tin (425 g) of whole baby corn spears
450 g (approx.) or 2 x 250 g packs of rindless rib bacon
toothpicks

1. Wash and drain corn.
2. Roll bacon (about 1½–2 layers) onto corn spears and skewer with toothpick
3. BBQ to taste.
4. Serve with a tomato sauce dip.

This recipe is from Gary O'Gorman, Nhulunbuy, NT.

Whitlof Surprise

Cut the whitlofs in halves lengthwise.
Place a slice of ham and one of gruyère cheese
in between the halves.
Wrap in aluminium foil and bury in the hot
ashes of the BBQ until cooked.
(it's beautiful!)

The above recipe is from Lyliane de Lyon, Ashfield, NSW. Her son-in-law drew the picture.

SEAFOOD

This is hardly a recipe — it's just a way of doing fish. We do it often in the country. The primary reason is that it tastes wonderful and secondly it's quick, neat, tidy, and there's not much cleaning up.

Ingredients
Obviously to begin with, you need fish fillets — barramundi if you can get that. Failing that, flathead or whiting, or really whatever you prefer, but they're the ones I would recommend.
some tarragon — either in powder form or fresh
as many stalks of fresh asparagus as you think you might need
some spring onions — thinly sliced
lemon — thinly sliced

The secret in this is to seal the foil packets as tightly as you possibly can. You don't want wonderful juices running out, nor steam escaping. So make the packet in such a way that it's sealed with a double fold, along the top and the edges.

You just put the fillet of fish on a piece of foil, place some sliced spring onion on top of the fish (as much as you like), then cut the fibrous ends off the asparagus — the tough part you don't eat — cut the asparagus into pieces and put some on top of the fish, add a couple of slices of lemon, and then seal the little packet up. Do this for each fillet, place it on the barbecue and cook over medium coals (if you can control the heat) for about 15 minutes, maybe a little more, but you can check one packet and see if the fish is becoming tender.

When you have cooked it to your satisfaction, gently remove each fillet from the foil with a spatula, trying not to break the fish as you place it on the plate. Serve it with a simple salad and a crisp very cold white wine. I would recommend my own wine, Cloud Valley Semillon, which when very cold is very crisp and lively with a creamy oak flavour. If you're not a lover of semillon (although I don't know many people who aren't, particularly with seafood) you might like to try a Cloud Valley Sauvignon Blanc. It's crisp and fruity, with just a little bit of edge, but very refreshing.

This is so simple and you'll love it

J.

Scampi with Pernod

Ingredients
12 large scampi*
150 g melted butter
Pernod
1 small bunch of dill, chopped
3 spring onions, chopped

Method
Cut scampi in half and clean. Add half the butter to hot plate (medium heat) and lay scampi flesh side down. Cook for 1 minute then turn. Sprinkle over dill and spring onions and brush with remaining butter. Turn once more and cook for further 1–2 minutes. Turn and pour over Pernod which will flame off. Serve immediately.

* Remember not to over-cook the scampi. If you cannot get hold of any scampi, substitute with large king prawns.

Thanks "Pete"

This recipe courtesy of Doyle's Seafood Restaurant, Watsons Bay, NSW.

Barbecued Fish

Serves 4

1 whole fish or 4 fillets/cutlets of choice
1 tablespoon oil
juice 1 lemon
chopped fresh herbs of choice
salt and pepper to taste

1. Clean and scale whole fish or rinse fillets/cutlets and pat dry with paper towel. Brush some heavy duty foil with the oil and place the fish on it. Sprinkle with lemon juice, herbs and salt and pepper. Wrap up and seal parcel well.
2. Place on a grill or lightly oiled hot plate and barbecue until fish flakes easily with a fork. Cooking times vary but a general guide is to allow 20-25 minutes per kilogram for whole fish and 4-5 minutes each side for fillets and cutlets, depending on thickness, turning only once.
3. Firmer fleshed fish, such as tuna, can be barbecued directly on a lightly oiled hot plate over medium heat for 4-5 minutes each side or until cooked to taste.

Prawns on the Barbie

Serves 4

1 kg green king prawns
60 g butter
1 clove garlic, crushed
1 tablespoon finely chopped fresh parsley

1. Peel the prawns and remove the back vein.
2. Melt the butter in a small saucepan and saute the garlic for 2 minutes. Stir in the parsley. Brush prawns with butter mixture.
3. Barbecue prawns over low heat for 2-3 minutes or until firm and opaque, brushing with butter mixture as they cook. Don't overcook prawns or they will become tough.
4. Serve immediately with a green salad.

Right: Calamari with Chilli and Crab (top), recipe page 97; Ling Kebabs with Lemon and Bay Leaves (middle), recipe page 95; Prawns on the Barbie (front)

Whole Atlantic Salmon with Almond Sauce

Serves 4

1 whole Atlantic salmon, cleaned and gutted
1 tablespoon Dijon mustard
1 tablespoon dried dill leaf tips
salt and pepper to taste
30 g butter, melted
1 slice white bread, crusts removed
100 g blanched almonds
$1/2$ cup water
$1/2$ cup olive oil
2 tablespoons lemon juice

1. Weigh salmon to calculate cooking time, allowing 20–25 minutes per kilo. Wash the salmon inside and out and pat dry with paper towel. Smear the cavity with mustard and sprinkle with dill and salt and pepper. Place the salmon on a piece of heavy duty foil, large enough to wrap up the fish into a parcel. Drizzle butter over fish, fold foil over and secure tightly.
2. Place parcel on a lightly oiled barbecue hot plate and cook for calculated cooking time or until flesh flakes easily with a fork.
3. Meanwhile, place the bread, almonds and water in a food processor or blender. Process until chopped. With the motor running, gradually add the oil in a slow, steady stream. Place sauce into a bowl, stir in the lemon juice and season to taste with salt and pepper.
4. Serve the sauce with the salmon, accompanied by a crisp green salad.

Left: Whole Atlantic Salmon with Almond Sauce

Bugs in Lemon and Honey

~ 180 grms butter, melted
~ 6 tablespoons honey, warmed
~ 6 tablespoons lemon juice
~ 4 tablespoons fresh chives
~ 2 tablespoons fresh dill
~ 1.5 kgs bug tails

Remove shell from underside of tail, leaving top intact. Place on a tray, flesh side up. Chop chives and dill, combine with all other ingredients. Pour evenly over tails. Marinade. Cook slowly on back of shell until tender and meat is white. Turn to seal. ENJOY.
by K.L. Bode.

Recipe supplied by K.L. Bode, Emerald, QLD.

Ling Kebabs with Lemon and Bay Leaves

Serves 4

500 g ling fillets, cut into bite-size pieces
1/2 cup olive oil
grated rind 1 lemon
2 cloves garlic, crushed
salt and pepper to taste
bamboo skewers, soaked in water for 30 minutes
1 lemon, extra, sliced
2 zucchinis, cut into 3 cm pieces
4 yellow button squash, halved
12 fresh bay leaves

1. Place the ling in a bowl and pour over combined oil, lemon rind and garlic. Season with salt and pepper. Cover and refrigerate for 2 hours.
2. Drain fish and reserve marinade. Thread fish onto skewers alternately with the lemon slices, zucchini, squash and bay leaves. Brush with marinade and barbecue over medium heat for 2-3 minutes each side or until cooked to taste, brushing with marinade from time to time.
3. Serve kebabs with fresh herb bread and a salad made with slices of tomato and fresh basil leaves.

See picture on page 91.

BBQ Delight Hot Plate

Use thick fillets of fish, I suggest barramundi, gemfish, jewfish, Murray cod etc. They're delicious in parsley crumbs.

For 4 people
1 kg fish fillets (any of the above)
juice of 4 lemons
white wine—1 cup
eggs, lightly whipped—2
oil—1 tablespoon (to mix with eggs)
breadcrumbs, seasoned—1½ cups
lemon rind, grated—½ cup
parsley, finely chopped—½ cup
salt, rock or common cooking
white pepper
cooking oil (for use on hot plate)

Method
Cut fillets into sizeable neat portions and marinate in lemon juice and wine overnight in fridge. Remove when needed and first dry with clean towel.

Lightly whip the eggs with one tablespoon of oil. Mix breadcrumbs thoroughly with lemon rind, parsley and plenty of salt and pepper.

Dip fish pieces firstly in egg then coat them in breadcrumb mixture, ensuring it sticks to the fish—press firmly into the crumbs if necessary.

In the meantime, pour some cooking oil onto the hot plate and ensure the surface is hot and ready. Fry pieces on each side until breadcrumbs are a light golden brown—they cook very quickly. Serve with side salad—tomatoes and basil—DELICIOUS!!

From Tom McDermott, Gwynneville, Wollongong, NSW.

Calamari with Chilli and Crab

Serves 4

4 small whole calamari hoods
200 g crab meat, fresh or canned
$1/2$ cup cooked jasmine rice
1 small red chilli, seeded and chopped
1 tablespoon snipped fresh chives
1 tablespoon fish sauce
2 teaspoons soy sauce
1 teaspoon grated fresh ginger
2 tablespoons oil
1 teaspoon lemon juice

1. Wash the calamari hoods inside and out. Pat dry with paper towel. Combine the crab meat, rice, chilli, chives, fish sauce, soy sauce and ginger in a bowl. Divide mixture into 4 portions and spoon into calamari hoods. Close opening with a toothpick. Brush with some of the combined oil and lemon juice.
2. Barbecue over medium heat for 10 minutes, turning and basting with more lemon oil mixture while cooking.
3. Remove toothpicks and serve with a fresh garden salad.

See picture on page 91.

Dorinda Hafner's Baked Fish

Ingredients

3 tablespoons of ginger root, finely grated
4 cloves of garlic, finely chopped
2 red chilies, chopped into a pulp
as much salt as you'd like
4 fresh fillets of salmon or snapper or tuna (I'd recommend the snapper)
couple of teaspoons of butter
Dorinda says a teaspoon of garlic salt — I just have a teaspoon of those ground salts and spices

Mix the ginger root, garlic, chillies and salt altogether, then rub it over the fillets. Use the butter to grease up four pieces of foil, place one of the fillets on each, and sprinkle well with the salt and seasoning. Make a little parcel out of the foil — don't wrap too tight — and put on the barbecue. If you're using the Dream Barbecue, light two of the burners and put the fish over the area where there are no burners, shut the lid and leave them there for 25–30 minutes. If you want a little chilli sauce, by all means do it — I must say I've tried it and I found it beautiful with just boiled potatoes and salad, but it's up to you.

P.S. Dorinda's book is great — worth reading.

Recipe from my good friend Dorinda Hafner's book A Taste of Africa.

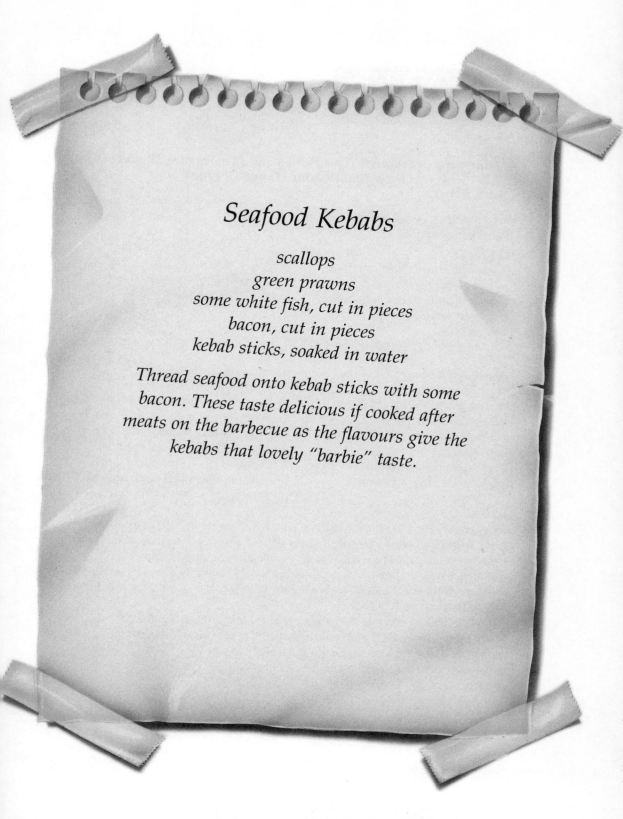

Seafood Kebabs

scallops
green prawns
some white fish, cut in pieces
bacon, cut in pieces
kebab sticks, soaked in water

Thread seafood onto kebab sticks with some bacon. These taste delicious if cooked after meats on the barbecue as the flavours give the kebabs that lovely "barbie" taste.

Recipe from Mrs Cathy McQuade, Geraldton, WA.

A PARK HYATT HOTEL

Barbecue Marinated Tiger Prawns on Lemongrass Skewers
with a Tomato and Mango Chutney

Serves 2

8 tiger prawns, peeled and cleaned
4 lemongrass sticks

Marinade
½ medium onion, sliced
1 clove garlic, crushed
½ hot red chilli, seeded and crushed
1 tablespoon olive oil
juice of 1 lime
salt and freshly ground black pepper

Tomato and Mango Chutney
¼ medium onion, diced
½ clove garlic, crushed
1 tablespoon olive oil
¼ teaspoon garam masala
¼ teaspoon cumin
1 tablespoon white wine
1 tablespoon mango vinegar

5 tablespoons tomato juice
½ tablespoon tomato paste
¼ teaspoon cinnamon
1 tablespoon castor sugar
1 mango, peeled and diced
2 tomatoes, peeled, seeded and diced
1 tablespoon sundried tomato, diced
salt and freshly ground black pepper

Method
To make the chutney: Using a medium pan, lightly sauté the diced onion and garlic in olive oil until softened. Add the ground ginger, garam masala and cook for a few minutes. Add the white wine, mango vinegar, tomato juice, tomato paste, cinnamon and castor sugar. Cook for 10 to 15 minutes over medium heat, then remove from the heat and add the mango, tomatoes and sundried tomato. Season to taste.

Cut the lemongrass into thin skewers then thread 2 prawns onto each lemongrass. Combine the marinade ingredients in a bowl. Add the prawn skewers and coat with the marinade. Let stand 1 to 2 hours.

Just before serving, cook the prawns on the barbecue over medium heat—make sure you don't overcook them as they will toughen.

Bon Appetit!

This recipe is from Stephane Foucher, Chef de Cuisine,
The Oak Room Restaurant, Hyatt Hotel Canberra, Yarralumla, ACT.

Prawns in Chilli Plum Sauce

Serves 4

1 kg green king prawns
$^1/_4$ cup olive oil
1 tablespoon chopped fresh coriander
1 clove garlic, crushed
1 tablespoon oil
2 shallots, finely chopped
1 clove garlic, extra, crushed
1 red chilli, seeded and finely chopped (or to taste)
825 g can dark plums, drained (juice reserved)
  pitted and pureed
2 tablespoons honey
1 tablespoon lemon juice
1 teaspoon grated fresh ginger
bamboo skewers, soaked in water for 30 minutes

1. Peel the prawns, leaving the tails intact. Remove the back vein. Place prawns in a bowl and pour over combined olive oil, coriander and garlic, turning to coat well. Cover and refrigerate for 2 hours.
2. Heat the oil in a saucepan and saute the shallots, garlic and chilli for 2 minutes. Stir in the plum puree, honey, lemon juice and ginger. Continue cooking for a further 3–4 minutes. Reduce heat and simmer for 15 minutes or until reduced and thickened. Cool slightly, then puree until smooth.
3. Drain the prawns. Thread onto skewers and barbecue over medium heat for 2–3 minutes or until they turn opaque. Don't overcook prawns or they will become tough.
4. Serve with the plum sauce, accompanied by steamed rice.

See picture on page 110.

Spicy Marinated BBQ Octopus with Fresh Papaya
Serves 6

Ingredients
2 kg octopus, cleaned and legs sectioned into two
Marinade
3 green chillies, discard seeds and chop finely
1 Spanish onion, peeled and chop finely
4 cloves garlic, peeled and chop finely
4 candle nuts or macadamia nuts
2 tablespoons of fresh diced ginger
1 teaspoon of turmeric
2 Kaffir lime leaves, sliced finely
2 stalks of lemongrass, sliced finely
salt and pepper
2 tablespoons of peanut oil

Method
Blend all marinade ingredients in the blender. Marinate the octopus for 1 hour. BBQ at medium to high temperature until octopus is nicely charred and tender, approximately 4–5 minutes.

To serve:
Serve with a little coconut cream and fresh papaya mixed with lime juice and coriander leaves.

Michael sent this recipe he knows I hate octopus J.

Thanks to Catalina Restaurant, Rose Bay, NSW.

Barramundi Kebabs with Apricots and Eggplant

Serves 4

$1/4$ cup olive oil
1 tablespoon chopped fresh basil
150 g dried apricots
$1/2$ cup white wine
$1/4$ cup hot water
1 kg barramundi fillets, cut into bite-size pieces
bamboo skewers, soaked in water for 30 minutes
4 baby eggplant, cut into 3 cm pieces
salt and pepper to taste

1. Place the oil and basil in a screw top jar, seal and shake well. Allow to stand for 2 hours.
2. Place the apricots in a bowl and pour on the white wine and water. Cover and allow to stand for 2 hours.
3. Thread barramundi onto skewers alternately with eggplant and drained apricots. Brush with basil some of the oil and season to taste with salt and pepper.
4. Barbecue over medium heat for 2–3 minutes each side, brushing with more basil oil as they cook.
5. Serve with potato salad and herb bread.

See picture on page 109.

freshKetch

Restaurant

Char-grilled John Dory Fillet with Seeded Mustard, Fresh Mint and Tomato Coulis
Recipe for 6 people

Tomato Coulis
10 *very ripe tomatoes*
1 *tspn tomato paste*
1 *handful fresh mint leaves*
1 *tspn sherry vinegar*
1 *red chilli*
2 *cloves garlic*
salt, pepper
2 *tblspn virgin olive oil*

Thank you George.
see you soon
JB

Roughly chop tomatoes and put in food processor. Add all ingredients except olive oil and blend for 4 minutes until smooth. Blend in virgin olive oil and strain through fine strainer. Heat through in a saucepan and keep warm on side while you prepare the fish.

Mustard Mix
6 *John Dory fillets*
1 *tblspn seeded mustard*
1 *tblspn Dijon mustard*
1 *tblspn chopped fresh mint*
1 *tblspn dry white wine*

Mix together mustards, mint and white wine. Take 6 nice fillets of John Dory and char-grill them on one side. Turn around and brush with mustard mix. When cooked serve with tomato coulis, green vegetables and salad.

This recipe is very light and fresh, full of flavour and perfect for a nice sunny day.

This recipe is from Olivier Massart, Chef, Fresh Ketch Restaurant, Mosman, NSW.

BBQ Garlic Apricot Prawns

You will need:

- fresh green prawns—the larger the better
- crushed garlic—fresh is best
- can of apricot nectar—approx. 700 mls
- splash of olive oil

You will do:

- Heat your BBQ plate until hot adding a splash of olive oil.
- Add the crushed garlic and toss until garlic browns slightly.
- Add the peeled green prawns and toss with the garlic until cooked—this takes 5 to 7 minutes.
- Pour the apricot nectar over the prawns. Keep tossing the prawns until they are coated with the nectar.
- Allow the coating on the prawns to "caramelize" slightly.
- Remove and serve immediately.

To clean BBQ plate, allow to heat. Any remaining nectar will burn and flake, enabling it to be scraped off your plate.

Recipe and illustration supplied by John Stephenson, Boyne Island, QLD

Marinated Whiskery Shark in Jamacian Spices

1 kg whiskery shark, cut into 2 cm strips
1 star anise
1 tsp black peppercorns
2 cloves
4 cloves garlic
25 gms fresh ginger
50 gms sugar (palm or dark brown)
25 gms carrot peeled and chopped
25 gms red onion, peeled and chopped

25 gms celery, peeled and chopped
6 hot chillies
1 bunch fresh coriander, including roots
1 lemon, zested and juiced
50 mls soy sauce
250 mls cider vinegar
salt and pepper
500 mls boiling water

1. Blend all ingredients (except water and fish) with soy sauce and cider vinegar till they form a paste—it will still be quite rough in consistency. You can add or reduce the chillies to vary the degree of spice.
2. Pour into a plastic container and pour over the hot water. Allow to cool and infuse.
3. Add the strips of shark to the marinade. Allow to marinate for at least 24 hours.
4. Char-grill over coals or scented wood, basting with the marinade. It can also be cooked on a flat grill plate, again basting frequently.

Papaya Salsa
250 gms papaya (paw-paw)
1/2 fresh grated coconut and its milk
1 bunch coriander
squeeze of lemon
100 gms Lebanese cucumber

1. Clean, skin and pip papaya. Cut into small dice.
2. Cut cucumber into small dice.
3. Mix together all other ingredients and fold into papaya and cucumber. Chill for 1 hour.

Serve shark on a bed of salad leaves, topped with a spoonful of the chilled papaya salsa and garnished with coriander leaves.

I picked this recipe up whilst working in Jamaica and I have successfully used it since on my menus and also at home for barbeques and parties. As an alternative baby octopus can be used—the marinade makes it very tender.

From Wayne Booth, Executive Chef, Verandah's Restaurant, Araluen Country Club, Roleystone, WA.

Blue-eye Cod Cutlets with a Hoisin Baste

Serves 4

4 blue-eye cod or kingfish cutlets
$1/4$ cup hoisin sauce
rind and juice 1 small lemon
1 tablespoon tomato sauce
2 teaspoons soy sauce
2 teaspoons honey
$1/4$ teaspoon lemon pepper

1. Place cutlets in a shallow dish. Combine the hoisin sauce, lemon rind and juice, tomato sauce, soy sauce, honey and lemon pepper in a bowl. Pour over fish, turning to coat. Cover and refrigerate for 2 hours.
2. Drain fish and reserve marinade. Barbecue fish on a lightly oiled hot plate for 4–5 minutes each side or until fish flakes when tested with a fork, brushing with marinade as it cooks.
3. Serve cutlets with char-grilled vegetables and salad.

See picture on page 110.

Tuna with Cucumber
Sour Cream Sauce

Serves 4

4 tuna steaks
2 tablespoons oil
2 teaspoons lemon pepper
1/2 cup sour cream
1/4 cup whole egg mayonnaise
1 tablespoon lemon juice
1 small cucumber, peeled, seeded and finely chopped
1 tablespoon chopped fresh dill
salt and white pepper to taste

1. Brush tuna steaks with oil and sprinkle with lemon pepper. Barbecue on a lightly oiled hot plate for 4–5 minutes each side or until cooked to taste.
2. Meanwhile, combine the sour cream, mayonnaise, lemon juice, cucumber and dill in a bowl. Season to taste with salt and pepper.
3. Serve tuna with the sour cream sauce, accompanied by a mixed leaf salad.

Right: Tuna with Cucumber Sour Cream Sauce (left);
Barramundi Kebabs with Apricots and Eggplant (right), recipe page 103

Whole Snapper Seasoned with Ginger, Soy and Shallots

Serves 4

4 plate-size snapper, cleaned and gutted
4 shallots, finely chopped
1 tablespoon chopped fresh coriander leaves
1 tablespoon chopped fresh mint
1 tablespoon soy sauce
2 teaspoons white wine vinegar
1 teaspoon grated fresh ginger
1 small chilli, seeded and chopped
salt and pepper to taste

1. Cut two slashes diagonally on each side of the fish to prevent curling during cooking. Combine the shallots, coriander, mint, soy sauce, vinegar, ginger and chilli in a bowl. Season to taste with salt and pepper. Spoon a quarter of this mixture into the cavity of each fish. Close opening with a toothpick. Loosely wrap fish in foil.
2. Barbecue on a lightly oiled hot plate for 5–7 minutes each side or until flesh flakes easily with a fork.
3. Serve with jacket potatoes and a green salad.

Left: Prawns in Chilli Plum Sauce (top), recipe page 101;
Whole Snapper Seasoned with Ginger, Soy and Shallots (middle);
Blue-eye Cod Cutlets with an Hoison Baste (front), recipe page 107

Not easy but worth the effort. J.

Involtini di Pesce Spada alla Griglia

Swordfish fillets rolled with herbs and zest, served with a tomato salsa

Serves 4

MEZZALUNA

Ingredients

800 g swordfish
1 whole orange
3 tablespoons parsley
1 tablespoon oregano
1 tablespoon marjoram
1 stalk rosemary
30 g Aeolian capers, dried in salt
2 stems shallots

2 cloves garlic
24 anchovy fillets
100 ml olive oil
4 whole tomatoes
1 small red onion
100 ml extra virgin olive oil
1 bunch arugola (rocket)
1 whole lemon
5 g black pepper, finely ground

Method

Cut 12 swordfish steaks (3 slices each portion), approximately 1½ cm thick. Grate the zest from orange and chop the herbs finely. Wash the capers and squeeze dry then chop finely. Mix the zest, capers, herbs and finely chopped shallots and minced garlic.

Lay the swordfish portions out flat, coat liberally with the herb mix and place 2 anchovy fillets on each. Roll the fish into tight tubes and secure with a toothpick.

To cook the involtini: brush with olive oil and cook over a charcoal grill, brushing occasionally with olive oil, for approximately 10 minutes.

For salsa: remove the flesh from the tomato and dice finely. Finely dice the red onion and mix with the diced tomato and 50 ml of extra virgin olive oil. Set aside.

To serve: arrange the involtini on a hot plate. Make a mound from the tomato salsa. Pour remaining olive oil around plate. Garnish with arugola and lemon wedges.

This is a good restaurant. J.

This recipe sent from Mezzaluna Restaurant, Potts Point, NSW.

Gourmet Fillet with Port Glaze
Serves four

Ingredients
1 whole cleaned eye fillet
1 whole crayfish
250 ml beef stock
100 ml port
4 bamboo skewers

Method

Divide fillet into four cuts and make incision in one end. Cut crayfish in half and remove tail meat, cut tail into quarters length ways, remove legs and save. Pocket craymeat into fillet and secure with bamboo skewer. Combine beef stock and port in a shall dish and marinate steaks four 1 to 2 hours.

To cook: Remove steaks from marinade and reduce stock until slightly thick. Char-grill steaks medium rare.

To serve: Remove steaks and slice into medallions. Arrange on warm plate spoon over port glaze, serve with seasonal vegetables and potato. Garnish with cray leg.

This recipe is from The Astor Grill Restaurant, Hobart, TAS.

Spicy Barbecued Octopus

Serves 4–6

For maximum flavour, marinate octopus overnight. Uncooked octopus can be frozen in marinade for up to 2 months.

1 kg baby octopus
1 clove garlic, crushed
2 teaspoons grated fresh ginger
1 tablespoon dry sherry
2 tablespoons tomato paste
2 teaspoons brown vinegar
1 teaspoon oil
2 teaspoons dark soya sauce
1 tablespoon honey

Prepare each octopus by cutting off head just below eye level, remove beak; rinse octopus under cold water. Combine remaining ingredients in bowl, add all octopus and mix well. Cover and refrigerate at least 12 hours turning occasionally. Barbecue octopus until tender. Absolutely delicious!

This recipe is from Megan Doohan, St Andrews, NSW.

Stuffed Baby Barramundi

Ingredients:
6 plate size barramundi, cleaned and gutted
6 cloves fresh garlic
olive oil

Stuffing:
4 slices of white bread, crust removed
½ cup milk
1 cup green prawn meat
1 cup calimari rings
1 cup scallops
1 medium onion, finely chopped
2 cloves finely chopped garlic
juice of 1 fresh lemon
salt and pepper to taste
3 tablespoons of freshly chopped chives or parsley

Begin by making 3 small incisions on each side of the cleaned barramundi. When this has been done to all the fish, allow 1 clove of garlic per fish, cut the garlic, place a small amount in each cut. Season the inside of the fish and set aside.

To make the stuffing, roughly chop slices of bread and add enough milk to make moist but not soggy. Set aside in a bowl for later. In another bowl, add roughly chopped prawn meat, calamari, and scallops. Add finely chopped onion and garlic, and lemon juice. Combine well. Squeeze any excess milk from bread and add to rest of ingredients. Combine well and add salt and pepper to taste.

Fill the cavity of the fish with this stuffing and season the outside of the fish. Put in the fridge for at least ½ hour before cooking. These fish can be prepared one or two days prior to your BBQ. To cook, oil the BBQ plate well and place fish on the plate, turning only once to cook the other side. Cook each side for about 10–12 minutes. BBQ should be on a low to medium heat so as not to cook the fish too quickly.

This recipe is from Darcy's Restaurant, Paddington, NSW.

Barbecued Whole Trout

Serves 4

4 x 250 g trout
1 tablespoon ground sweet paprika
salt to taste
1 small lemon, finely sliced
1 tablespoon chopped fresh tarragon
2 tablespoons dry white wine
60 g butter, melted

1. Make two slashes diagonally on each side of each trout. Sprinkle cavities and skin with combined paprika and salt. Place lemon slices inside cavities with a teaspoon of chopped tarragon in each. Sprinkle with wine.
2. Brush fish with melted butter and barbecue over medium heat for 4-5 minutes each side or until flesh flakes easily with a fork.
3. Serve with a salad made from tomato slices and fresh mint leaves.

Dear Mr Laws,

My husband and I just love your radio program. We are professional fishers in the Stanage Bay, Shoal Water Bay area, north of Rockhampton.

I have a recipe you just may be interested in. We love it and so does every other person I pass it on to. It's quick, easy and tasty!

BBQ Barramundi Wings

4 Barra wings (other large fish wings may be substituted)
lemon pepper seasoning
salt
microwave
cooking oil
barbecue

Give the Barra wings a healthy coating of lemon pepper seasoning and salt. Microwave for 5 to 8 minutes, depending on size of wings and microwave. Then throw on the BBQ with a bit more seasoning, a touch of cooking oil and salt. Cook until golden on both sides. Serve with fresh salad and tasty cooked Queensland mud crab.

Talk about melt in your mouth! This recipe is worthy of any taste buds.

Thank you to Mrs Vonni Ireland, Stanage Bay, QLD.

CHICKEN

Pollo Griglia a la Lago de Como

Grilled chicken a la Lake Como

Once when we were staying at Villa D'Este at Lake Como, we took a boat and travelled to an island famous for its chickens. It's fame was rightly earned — this is the simplest and best grilled chicken I have ever had.

How to make it

You need a good quality small chicken, cut in half. If you can get a free range one, do, but try and avoid a frozen one. If it's not cut in half, cut it yourself and beat it flat. I always find an old meat cleaver is good for beating flat — obviously not the sharp edge, the side is what you use because it's got some weight in it and it's large. It's also handy to have around the house.

So now you have two halves of chicken, flattened out. Marinate the chicken with some lemon juice, pepper and some garlic (plenty of garlic) for a couple of hours, moving it around every now and again. You can put some chilli in if you like, but I'm inclined to think it over-does it.

When you're ready to cook, sprinkle it with salt and put it on a medium grill with the skin side of the half chicken towards the fire. Let it cook until that skin has turned a light browny colour then turn it over on the other side. All the time you're doing this you can baste it with the lemon juice and liquid that's left. After about 15 minutes on that side, turn it over and cook it again, keep turning and cooking and tipping the marinade on. If you run out of the marinade, drizzle on a little olive oil every now and again. It could take 40–45 minutes to complete cooking. Make sure it's cooked as there's nothing worse than under-cooked chicken. You can pierce it and make sure there's no pinkness near the bone.

Serve it with a good white wine — if the Rosemount Show Reserve Chardonnay is not out of your reach then that's the one I recommend. I really believe it's the best all-round white wine on the Australian market.

Darling John,

Here is the chicken wing recipe you asked me for

All my love
Gabrielle.

Barbecued Chicken Wings.

1 green paw-paw.
chicken wings.
fresh red chilli (chopped finely)
palm sugar.
shoyu (soy sauce)
garlic crushed.

Peel and chop into cubes and blend green paw-paw. Marinate chicken wings in paw-paw for ½ hour (this is a meat tenderizer). Wipe off paw-paw place wings in a marinade of the other ing. proportion's adjusted to taste). Marinate 1-2 hours. Place on grill or barbecue to cook.

This recipe is from my daughter Gabrielle.

Satay Chicken

Serves 4

500 g chicken breast fillets, cut into bite-size pieces

$1/4$ cup coconut cream

2 tablespoons peanut butter

2 tablespoons tahini (sesame seed paste)

2 tablespoons lemon juice

1 tablespoon oil

1 small red chilli, seeded and finely chopped

1 clove garlic, crushed

salt and pepper to taste

bamboo skewers, soaked in water for 30 minutes

1 red capsicum, seeded and cut into large squares

1 green capsicum, seeded and cut into large squares

1. Place chicken in a bowl. Combine the coconut cream, peanut butter, tahini, lemon juice, oil, chilli and garlic in a bowl. Season to taste with salt and pepper. Pour over chicken and mix to coat well. Cover and refrigerate for at least 4 hours or overnight.

2. Thread chicken pieces and capsicum alternately onto skewers. Barbecue on a grid over medium heat for 10–15 minutes or until cooked through.

3. Serve with steamed rice.

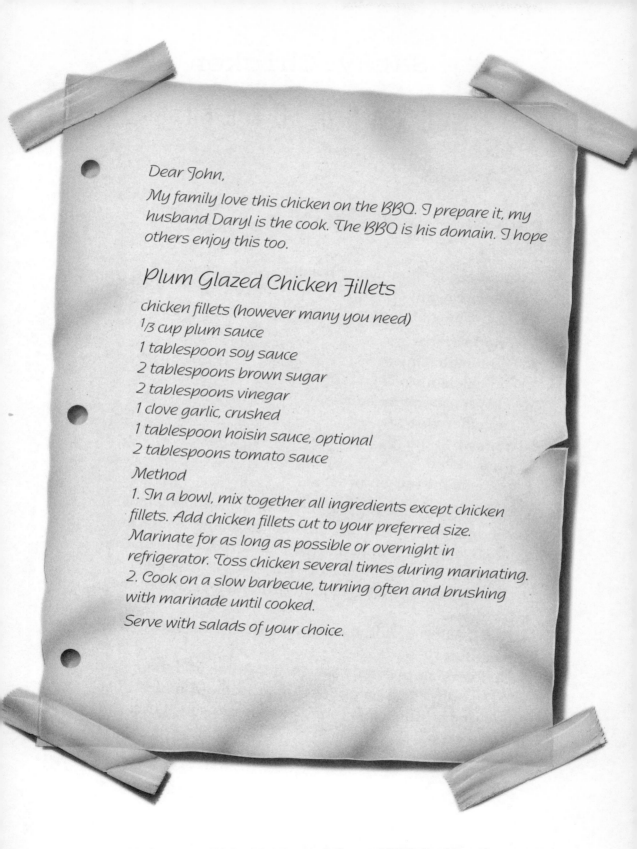

Dear John,

My family love this chicken on the BBQ. I prepare it, my husband Daryl is the cook. The BBQ is his domain. I hope others enjoy this too.

Plum Glazed Chicken Fillets

chicken fillets (however many you need)
1/3 cup plum sauce
1 tablespoon soy sauce
2 tablespoons brown sugar
2 tablespoons vinegar
1 clove garlic, crushed
1 tablespoon hoisin sauce, optional
2 tablespoons tomato sauce

Method

1. In a bowl, mix together all ingredients except chicken fillets. Add chicken fillets cut to your preferred size. Marinate for as long as possible or overnight in refrigerator. Toss chicken several times during marinating.
2. Cook on a slow barbecue, turning often and brushing with marinade until cooked.

Serve with salads of your choice.

Thanks to Mrs Lesley Honeysett, Gulgong, NSW, for this recipe.

GRAND ORBIT

BBQ Chicken Burritto
Serves 4

400 g chicken (thigh meat), boneless and skinless
1 tablespoon chives, sliced
4 x 15 cm (6 inch) flour tortillas

Marinade/Sauce
200 ml tomato sauce
200 ml chicken stock
50 ml Worcestershire sauce
100 ml cider vinegar
50 g brown sugar
1 onion, sliced
1 teaspoon mustard powder

1. Mix all marinade ingredients well. Cover chicken with marinade, place in an airtight container and steep overnight.
2. Remove chicken from marinade and reduce marinade carefully in saucepan on stove till sauce consistency.
3. Cook chicken on BBQ or char-grill, remove and allow to cool slightly.
4. Shred chicken. Add the chives and enough sauce to bind the mixture.
5. Divide mixture evenly between tortillas, roll them up and slice in half. Place on plate with guacamole, a nice fresh salad and a little sour cream. Place extra sauce in a jug and serve.

Recipe from Ross Howell, Executive Chef, Grand Orbit Restaurant, Brisbane, QLD.

Chicken with Apricot Ginger Sauce

Serves 4

4 chicken breast fillets
1 tablespoon oil
salt and white pepper to taste
1 cup apricot jam
30 g butter, cubed
2 tablespoons lemon juice
1 teaspoon freshly grated ginger
2 tablespoons sherry

1. Brush chicken fillets with oil. Season to taste with salt and pepper. Barbecue over medium heat for 15-20 minutes each side or until cooked to taste.
2. Meanwhile, place the apricot jam in a small saucepan over gentle heat and stir in the butter, lemon juice and ginger. Simmer gently for 2 minutes. Remove from heat and stir in the sherry.
3. Serve chicken with the sauce, accompanied by steamed broccoli and carrots.

Savoury Chicken Wings

2 kg chicken wings
2 chicken stock cubes
1 large onion, chopped
water to cover chicken wings in large boiler

Marinade
½ cup thin soy sauce
½ teaspoon sugar
3 cloves garlic
1 teaspoon salt
3 tablespoons hoisin sauce
3 tablespoons sweet sherry
¾ cup vegetable oil

Cook chicken wings in large boiler with the stock cubes, chopped onion and water for about 20 minutes, or until just tender. Drain and let cool. (Keep this stock to make some chicken soup.)

Combine all the other ingredients and add the cooled chicken wings. Let stand at least 1 hour (best left overnight), turning occasionally to marinate all the wings.

Cover a wire rack with aluminium foil and put into a baking dish. Place chicken wings on wire rack and cook over moderate heat until nicely browned, approximately 20 minutes.

This recipe is from Joan Summerside, Port Kembla, NSW.

Barbecue Chicken and Prawns

Serves 4 to 6

4 chicken breast fillets or 8 chicken thigh fillets
500 g peeled and deveined green prawns, tails intact

Marinade

½ cup dry white wine
1 tablespoon Thai green curry powder
¼ cup olive oil
2 cloves garlic, crushed
1 teaspoon grated lemon rind
freshly ground pepper

Mix all the ingredients for the marinade, add the chicken and prawns, cover and refrigerate. Leave for 2 to 3 hours.

Very lightly oil the hot plate/barbecue grill. Place the chicken on the barbecue and cook over hot coals, turning to cook on both sides until golden brown and cooked through. Add the prawns last because they only take a few minutes to cook.

Serve with rice and green salad.

This recipe is from Sue Foley, Armidale, NSW.

Chicken with Capsicum and Glazed Onions

Serves 4

4 chicken breast fillets, cut into bite-size pieces
$1/4$ cup tomato paste
2 tablespoons honey
1 tablespoon soy sauce
1 teaspoon freshly grated ginger
cracked black pepper to taste
12 small pickling onions, peeled
60 g butter, melted
bamboo skewers, soaked in water for 30 minutes
1 large red capsicum, seeded and cut into large squares

1. Place chicken in a bowl. Combine the tomato paste, honey, soy sauce and ginger. Season to taste with pepper. Pour over chicken and mix well to coat evenly. Cover and refrigerate for at least 4 hours or overnight.
2. Meanwhile, parboil the onions for 5 minutes, drain well and pat dry with paper towel. Saute in melted butter over high heat for 2–3 minutes. Remove from heat and cool.
3. Drain chicken and reserve marinade. Thread chicken onto skewers alternately with the onions and capsicum. Barbecue over medium heat for 10–15 minutes or until cooked through, turning and basting with marinade while cooking.
4. Serve with a rice salad and crusty bread.

Right: Barbecued Sweet Corn (top), recipe page 156; Barbecued Chicken with Mango Salsa (middle), recipe page 134; Chicken with Capsicum and Glazed Onions (front)

Chicken Parcels with Bacon and Corn

Serves 4

4 chicken breast fillets
2 rashers rindless bacon, finely chopped
1 onion, finely chopped
310 g can corn kernels, drained
2 tablespoons white wine
cracked black pepper to taste

1. Place each chicken breast on a square of heavy duty foil. Top with bacon, onion and corn. Sprinkle each fillet with 2 teaspoons of white wine and cracked black pepper to taste. Fold up foil into tight, neat parcels.
2. Cook parcels over medium heat, turning once, for 15–20 minutes each side. Open parcels on a serving plate to enjoy the aroma.
3. Serve with jacket potatoes and sour cream.

Left: Tasty Chicken Drumsticks (top), recipe page 132; Chicken Parcels with Bacon and Corn (middle); Chicken Thighs with Redcurrant Glaze (front), recipe page 130

Chicken Thighs with Redcurrant Glaze

Serves 4

1 cup red wine
4 shallots, finely chopped
1 stalk celery, chopped
2 parsley stalks
2 sprigs thyme
2 bay leaves
salt and pepper to taste
8 chicken thigh fillets
$1/2$ cup redcurrant jelly, melted

1. Combine the red wine, shallots, celery, parsley, thyme and bay leaves in a bowl. Season to taste with salt and pepper.
2. Place chicken in a shallow dish and pour red wine mixture over. Cover and refrigerate for at least 4 hours or overnight.
3. Drain chicken and reserve marinade. Barbecue over medium heat for 10–15 minutes. Brush chicken with some of the melted redcurrant jelly and continue cooking for a further 10–15 minutes, turning and brushing with more redcurrant jelly from time to time.
4. Add any remaining redcurrant jelly to strained marinade in a small saucepan. Bring to the boil and reduce by a third.
5. Serve chicken with the redcurrant sauce, accompanied by jacket potatoes and a green salad.

See picture on page 128.

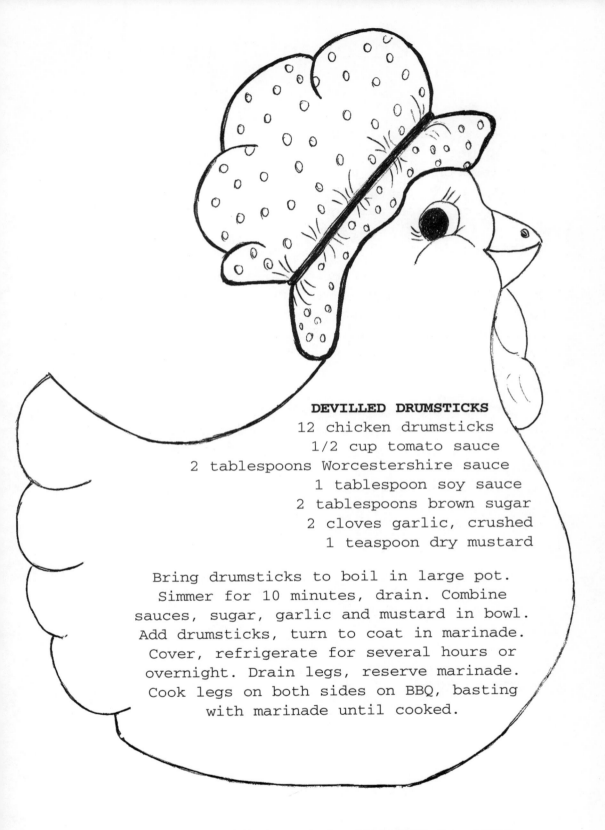

DEVILLED DRUMSTICKS

12 chicken drumsticks
1/2 cup tomato sauce
2 tablespoons Worcestershire sauce
1 tablespoon soy sauce
2 tablespoons brown sugar
2 cloves garlic, crushed
1 teaspoon dry mustard

Bring drumsticks to boil in large pot.
Simmer for 10 minutes, drain. Combine
sauces, sugar, garlic and mustard in bowl.
Add drumsticks, turn to coat in marinade.
Cover, refrigerate for several hours or
overnight. Drain legs, reserve marinade.
Cook legs on both sides on BBQ, basting
with marinade until cooked.

Recipe and illustration from Mrs Heather Colvin, Wilberforce, NSW.

Tasty Chicken Drumsticks

Serves 4

grated rind and juice 1 lemon
$^1/_4$ cup white wine
1 tablespoon German mustard
1 teaspoon Worcestershire sauce
1 teaspoon dried tarragon
salt and pepper to taste
8 chicken drumsticks

1. Combine the lemon rind and juice, wine, mustard, Worcestershire sauce and tarragon in a bowl. Season to taste with salt and pepper.
2. Place drumsticks in a shallow dish and pour marinade over, turning chicken in marinade to coat well.
3. Cover and refrigerate for at least 4 hours or overnight.
4. Drain chicken and reserve marinade. Barbecue drumsticks on a grid over medium heat for 20–30 minutes or until cooked through turning and basting with marinade.
5. Serve with salad and crusty bread.

See picture on page 128.

Spicy Chicken Kebabs

1 kg chicken breasts, boned and skinned
2 large white onions
2 large red capsicums
1 x 440 g tin pineapple pieces in natural juice (reserve juice for marinade)
Bamboo skewers, soaked in water for 1 hour to prevent burning

Marinade
3 tablespoons peanut butter
2 tablespoons dry sherry
reserved pineapple juice
1 teaspoon green curry powder
$1/2$ teaspoon chilli powder

Cut chicken into one inch cubes. Cut onion and capsicum into squares. Thread chicken, onion, capsicum and pineapple onto skewers. Make up marinade — it needs plenty of stirring until smooth. Marinate for at least 2 hours. Grill over slow coals.

This recipe is from Verna Pearce, Narrikup, WA.

Barbecued Chicken with Mango Salsa

Serves 4

30 g butter
2 shallots, finely chopped
1 small red chilli, seeded and finely chopped
425 g can sliced mango, drained and chopped
grated rind and juice $1/2$ lemon
2 tablespoons chopped fresh coriander
4 chicken breast fillets
1 tablespoon oil
salt and pepper to taste

1. Melt the butter in a saucepan and saute the shallots and chilli until softened. Add the mango and cook over a low heat for 2-3 minutes. Add the lemon rind and juice and coriander. Remove from heat and keep warm.
2. Brush chicken with oil and sprinkle with salt and pepper. Barbecue over medium heat for 15-20 minutes each side or until cooked through.
3. Serve with the mango salsa, accompanied by a green salad.

See picture on page 127.

Pier
ROSE BAY
94 NEW SOUTH HEAD ROAD · ROSE BAY 2029
PHONE 327 4187 · 327 6561

Char-grilled Breast of Guinea Fowl with Beetroot Relish

Ingredients: (6 portions)

6 pieces guinea fowl supreme with skin left on
100 ml demi glace
red wine vinegar
salt and pepper
sauteed potatoes (6 portions)

Beetroot Relish

1 kg beetroot, peeled and shredded
½ kg brown sugar
½ litre red wine vinegar
250 gm raisins
½ teaspoon chilli puree

Method:

Place all ingredients into a pot and bring to the boil. Lower to simmer and cook till liquid has nearly evaporated, approximately 2 hours. Allow to completely cool and store in sterilized jars.

Brush the breast of guinea fowl with butter, season with salt and pepper and grill. Make sure the guinea fowl is kept moist and a little pink inside.

Place the guinea fowl breast on the plate and garnish with a mound of beetroot relish. Heat demi glace and spoon over guinea fowl.

Serve with sauteed potatoes.

If you find this too hard — go to the "Pier" — come to think of it I'll go to the "Pier" anyway — it would! K.

From Pier Restaurant, Rose Bay, NSW.

KETTLE BARBECUING AND SPIT ROASTING

Beef with a Garlic Butter Baste

Serves 4-6

$1^1/2$ kg topside roast (see Note)
fresh rosemary sprigs
1 tablespoon oil
salt and pepper to taste
100 g butter, melted
2 cloves garlic, crushed
$1/4$ cup finely chopped fresh parsley

1. With a sharp knife, make small incisions in the meat and insert the rosemary sprigs. Push the spit through the centre of the meat and secure with the holding forks. Place a drip tray on the grid under the meat. Brush meat with oil and season with salt and pepper. Spit roast meat for $1^1/2$ hours or until cooked to taste.
2. Meanwhile, combine the butter, garlic and parsley. Baste beef with butter mixture every 10 minutes during the last 30 minutes.
3. Allow to stand for 10-15 minutes before carving. Serve with roast potatoes, pumpkin and peas.

Note: Choose a roast with an even shape to ensure uniform cooking.

Standing Rib Roast

Serves 4–6

1^1/$_2$ kg standing rib roast
^{1}/$_2$ cup oil
salt and cracked black pepper to taste
6 potatoes, peeled and halved
^{1}/$_2$ small butternut pumpkin, peeled and cut into large chunks
6 baby eggplant, halved lengthwise
6 zucchinis, halved lengthwise

1. Place a drip tray in the coals below the grid of a kettle barbecue. Brush the roast with some of the oil and sprinkle with salt and pepper. Place on the grid and close the lid. Cook for 1^1/$_2$ hours or until cooked to taste, brushing with more oil from time to time to keep the beef moist.
2. Prepare the potatoes and pumpkin. Brush with oil and place in separate foil trays. When the beef has cooked for 30 minutes, place the foil trays onto the grid beside the beef. Close the lid and continue cooking.
3. Brush eggplant and zucchini with oil and place directly on the barbecue grid 10 minutes before the end of cooking. Turn after 5 minutes.
4. Allow roast to stand for 10–15 minutes before carving.
5. Serve with the vegetables, accompanied by gravy of your choice and store-bought horseradish cream.

Garlic Lamb with a Herb Sauce

Serve 4-6

1 leg of lamb
2 cloves garlic, sliced
$1/3$ cup mild mustard of choice
1 tablespoon chopped fresh mint
1 teaspoon dried thyme
1 teaspoon dried rosemary

1. Weigh the lamb to calculate the cooking time, allowing 30 minutes per 500 g. With a sharp knife make small incisions in the meat and insert a slice of garlic in each.
2. Combine the mustard, mint, thyme and rosemary and spread over lamb.
3. Place a drip tray in the coals of a kettle barbecue below the grid. Place lamb on the grid, close the lid and cook for calculated cooking time or until cooked to taste.
4. Allow to stand for 10-15 minutes before carving.
5. Serve with rice and salad.

Lamb Racks with a Basil and Pine Nut Crust

Serves 4–6

100 g butter, melted
1 cup fresh breadcrumbs
$^1/_4$ cup chopped fresh basil
$^1/_4$ cup chopped fresh parsley
$^1/_4$ cup pine nuts, toasted and chopped
2 tablespoons grated parmesan cheese
2 racks lamb, each with 6 cutlets
salt and pepper to taste

1. Combine the butter, breadcrumbs, basil, parsley, pine nuts and parmesan.
2. Season the lamb with salt and pepper, then press the breadcrumb mixture onto the backs of the racks.
3. Place a drip tray in the coals of a kettle barbecue below the grid. Place lamb racks on the grid, close the lid and cook for 35–40 minutes or until cooked to taste.
4. Allow to stand for 10 minutes before cutting into cutlets.
5. Serve with sauteed potatoes, carrots and peas.

Lamb with Mushrooms and Mint

Serves 4-6

1 leg lamb, boned
2 cloves garlic, sliced
125 g ham, chopped
125 g button mushrooms, finely chopped
$1/2$ cup fresh breadcrumbs
$1/4$ cup chopped fresh mint
1 tablespoon oil
salt and pepper to taste

1. Weigh lamb to calculate cooking time, allowing 30 minutes per 500 g. Lay out on a flat surface. With a sharp knife, make small incisions in the meat. Insert a slice of garlic into each cut.
2. Combine the ham, mushrooms, breadcrumbs and mint. Spread over lamb and roll up. Secure tightly with string. Brush with oil and season to taste with salt and pepper.
3. Place a drip tray in the coals of a kettle barbecue below the grid. Place lamb on the grid, close the lid and cook for calculated cooking time or until cooked to taste.
4. Allow to stand for 10-15 minutes before carving.
5. Serve with a salad of mixed leaves, tomatoes, fetta cheese and olives.

Spit Roasted Pork

Serves 4-6

1^1/$_2$ kg boned and rolled loin of pork
^{1}/$_2$ cup oil
^{1}/$_4$ cup white wine
1 tablespoon lemon juice
1 teaspoon dried thyme
^{1}/$_2$ teaspoon dried sage
2 bay leaves

1. Place the pork in a baking dish. Combine the oil, white wine, lemon juice, thyme, sage and bay leaves in a bowl. Pour over pork. Cover and refrigerate for 2 hours, basting with marinade from time to time.
2. Drain pork and reserve marinade. Place pork on the spit and secure with holding forks. Place a drip tray under the meat. Spit roast for 1^1/$_2$ hours or until cooked through, basting with marinade from time to time.
3. Allow to stand for 10-15 minutes before carving.
4. Serve with coleslaw and potato salad (see page 155).

Spit Roasted Chicken

Serves 4-6

1 x No 18 chicken
$1/4$ cup oil
grated rind and juice 1 lemon
1 tablespoon chopped fresh tarragon, or 1 teaspoon dried
salt and pepper to taste

1. Wash the chicken inside and out and pat dry with paper towel. Tie the chicken together with string and cover wings tips and drumstick knuckles with foil. Place on a spit and secure with holding forks. Brush with combined oil, lemon rind and juice, tarragon and salt and pepper.
2. Place a drip tray on the grid under the chicken and spit roast for $1-1^1/2$ hours, basting with lemon tarragon mixture from time to time.
3. Allow to stand for 10 minutes before carving.
4. Serve with corn cobs and glazed carrots.

Christmas Turkey Cooked on the Barbecue

Serves 6–8

1 turkey
3 cups fresh breadcrumbs
1 onion, finely chopped
1 stalk celery, finely chopped
375 g peeled roasted chestnuts, chopped (see Note)
$1/4$ cup chopped fresh parsley
1 tablespoon brandy
1 tablespoon snipped fresh chives
$1/4$ teaspoon dried mixed herbs
1 egg, lightly beaten
$1/4$ cup oil

1. Wash turkey inside and out and pat dry thoroughly with paper towels.
2. Combine the breadcrumbs, onion, celery, chestnuts, parsley, brandy, chives and mixed herbs. Stir in the beaten egg and mix well.
3. Stuff turkey with breadcrumb mixture. Tie securely with string. Weigh the bird to calculate cooking time, allowing 40–45 minutes per kilogram.
4. Place a drip tray in the coals of a kettle barbecue below the grid. Brush turkey with oil and place on the grid, close the lid and cook for calculated cooking time, basting with oil from time to time. If bird is browning too quickly, cover with oiled foil.
5. Allow to stand for 20 minutes before carving.
6. Serve with store-bought cranberry sauce, and gravy and vegetables of your choice (see Note).

Note: Peeled roasted chestnuts are available in jars at most health food shops. Roast potatoes and pumpkin can be cooked in foil trays in the barbecue during the last hour of cooking, if desired.

SAUCES, MARINADES AND BASTES

Barbecue Sauce

Makes about 2 cups
2 tablespoons olive oil
1 large onion, chopped
1 cup beef stock
$1/2$ cup tomato sauce
2 tablespoons red wine vinegar
1 tablespoon honey
1 tablespoon Worcestershire sauce
$1/2$ tablespoon sweet chilli sauce
salt and pepper to taste

1. Heat the oil in a saucepan and saute the onion until tender. Add the stock, tomato sauce, vinegar, honey, Worcestershire and chilli sauces. Season to taste with salt and pepper. Cover and simmer for 5 minutes.
2. Place in a food processor and process until smooth.
3. Serve with steaks, chops and sausages.

Red Wine and Thyme Sauce

Serves 4
1 cup red wine
3 shallots, finely chopped
1 teaspoon dried thyme
1 cup beef stock
1 tablespoon brandy
1 tablespoon lemon juice
1 tablespoon finely chopped fresh parsley
1 tablespoon cornflour

1. Place the wine, shallots and thyme in a saucepan over medium heat. Bring to the boil, reduce heat and simmer until liquid reduces to $1/3$ cup.
2. Add the beef stock, brandy, lemon juice and parsley. Mix a little of this liquid into the cornflour and stir to form a smooth paste. Pour cornflour mixture into the sauce and stir well to combine. Bring to the boil, reduce heat and simmer until thickened.
3. Serve with beef steaks or lamb chops.

Swaggie's Sauce

1 TIN PUREED TOMATOES
1 TABLESPOON BUTTER
1 SMALL ONION, (GRATED)
1 TEASPOON SUGAR
¼ CUP RED WINE
¼ CUP WATER
¼ CUP VINEGAR
2 TABLESPOONS HONEY
1 CLOVE CRUSHED GARLIC

GENTLY WARM VINEGAR, WATER & HONEY
UNTIL COMBINED, THEN ADD GARLIC.

MELT THE BUTTER IN A HEAVY PAN
AND SAUTE ONION FOR 2-3 MINS.

ADD TOMATO PUREE, SUGAR, RED WINE,
AND WATER.

SIMMER GENTLY FOR 15-20 MINS.
UNTIL SAUCE HAS THICKENED.

David Tanare   Woy Woy N.S.W.

This recipe is from David Tanare, Woy Woy, NSW.

My favourite restaurant in Brisbane — thks Michael

Michael's Riverside Restaurants

Chicken and Seafood Baste Oriental

⅔ cup chopped green shallots
¼ cup Kikoman soy sauce
¼ cup dry sherry
2 tablespoons minced ginger
2 tablespoons chilli oil
2 teaspoons sesame oil
2 teaspoons five spice powder

Mix all together and baste on chicken or seafood while cooking.

Honey Mustard Sauce for Lamb

¼ cup Dijon mustard
1 teaspoon whole mustard seeds
1 teaspoon milled black peppercorns
3 tablespoons brandy
3 tablespoons chopped fresh tarragon
2 tablespoons olive oil
1½ tablespoons tarragon vinegar
1 tablespoon honey

Mix all together and baste on lamb while cooking.

Salmon/Tuna Marinade

½ cup finely diced Spanish (red) onion
2 cloves garlic, crushed
2 teaspoons caraway seeds
2 teaspoons ground coriander
½ teaspoon cayenne pepper
1 tablespoon olive oil
½ teaspoon salt

Mix all together and baste on fish prior to grilling.
Serve with a yoghurt sauce.

These recipes are from Michael's Riverside Restaurants, Brisbane, QLD.

Creamy Mushroom Sauce

Serves 4

60 g butter
250 g mushrooms, chopped
2 tablespoons brandy
300 ml cream
salt and pepper to taste

1. Melt the butter in a saucepan and saute the mushrooms over medium heat until softened, about 4 minutes. Stir in the brandy and cook, stirring, for a further 2 minutes. Stir in the cream and simmer until sauce reduces and thickens. Season to taste with salt and pepper.
2. Serve with chicken or beef.

Szechuan Hot Sauce

Serves 4

4 fresh red chillies, seeded and finely chopped
2 shallots, very finely chopped
$1/2$ cup soy sauce
$1/2$ cup chicken stock
$1/4$ cup red wine vinegar
1 tablespoon sesame oil

1. Combine all ingredients in a bowl.
2. Use as a dipping sauce for chicken. It will keep refrigerated for several days.

Lemon and Garlic Marinade for Beef

Makes about $3/4$ cup
$1/2$ cup olive oil
2 tablespoons red wine vinegar
rind and juice 1 lemon
1 clove garlic, crushed

1. Combine all ingredients. Pour over beef and marinate for at least 2 hours.
2. Brush marinade over beef while cooking.

JOHN LAWS COUNTRY SAUCES

In some of the excellent photography in this book, you'll notice some John Laws Country Sauces, which I've created in association with my friends at Barbeques Galore. The selection consists of the following six products and, believe me, they definitely add flavour to your barbecue enjoyment:

RED CENTRE HOT BBQ SAUCE ingredients: crushed tomatoes puree, vinegar, onion, soy sauce, spices, herbs, tomato paste, chilli and garlic.

My favourite BBQ sauce — it's terrific and I'm proud to say so.

TOP END TERIYAKI SESAME SAUCE ingredients: naturally brewed soy sauce, onions, garlic, sugar, honey, salt, ginger, sesame oil and sesame seeds.

Fair dinkum flavour - just superb

CLOUD VALLEY FARM DRESSING ingredients: vinegar, buttermilk, egg yolk, onion, vegetable oil, spices, herbs, salt, sugar, lemon juice and garlic.

So good, it makes anybody's salad taste terrific, even mine.

PROSERPINE PINEAPPLE CHILLI SAUCE ingredients: crushed pineapple, onions, pepper, spices, herbs, fresh chilli, garlic, ginger and vinegar.

If you love seafood, you'll love it even more with this sauce.

COASTAL COUNTRY MUSTARD ingredients: ground mustard seeds, salt, acetic acid, sugar, spices and herbs.

My own delicate blend of mustard, herbs and spices with a touch of honey.

TAMWORTH HOT LICK MUSTARD ingredients: ground mustard seeds, salt, acetic acid, sugar, spices and herbs.

For those who like it hot, this fiery mustard is the one you can't do without.

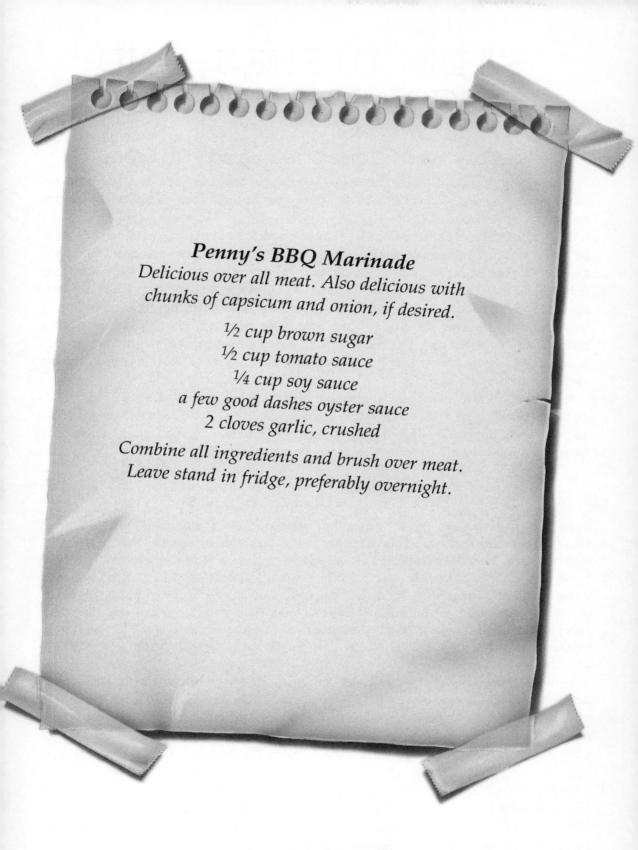

Penny's BBQ Marinade

Delicious over all meat. Also delicious with chunks of capsicum and onion, if desired.

½ cup brown sugar
½ cup tomato sauce
¼ cup soy sauce
a few good dashes oyster sauce
2 cloves garlic, crushed

Combine all ingredients and brush over meat. Leave stand in fridge, preferably overnight.

From Mrs Penny Carroll, Golden Beach, VIC.

SIDE DISHES AND ACCOMPANIMENTS

Barbecued Tomatoes and Onions

A good way of doing tomatoes and onions is in one of those hinged baskets — quite often they're used for fish — they're readily available.

Use a little of olive oil — use good quality if you can — and if you've got some rosemary use that too. Slice up the onions, fairly thickly, put in a dish and mix with the oil, cut up the tomato, lay in the basket along with the onion and put a few sprigs of rosemary on top. Grind on the salt and pepper together, or use the Sellou grinder that has the herbs. Then just put the basket on top of the barbecue. You need only grill them for about 3 minutes one side, and 3 minutes on the other. That's easy, tidy and works well.

PS: You could ring this number to find out the availability of Sellou products (02) 389 1993. In grinders, they have wonderful salts and peppers and lemon herb peppers. These also come in gourmet bags and refill bags. *See picture on page 20.*

Barbecued Potatoes

Take new potatoes, boil them for about 12–15 minutes, drain and toss them around with a bit of oil, grind on some Sellou salt and pepper and dried chilli pepper. Take a long skewer, thread five or six potatoes onto the skewer. Pour a little oil over them and pop them on the barbecue. Let them get a nice colour on the outside, because they'll be virtually cooked on the inside. Slide them off the skewer and onto a plate. I like them better in the coals. That's the real way to do them if you're in the bush.

You can use sweet potatoes if you like — they're wonderful. Give the potatoes a scrub if you feel inclined and lie them in the hot ashes. Then if you have a small shovel scoop a few more ashes over the top and bury them. They will probably need to sit there for about 45 minutes. Take them out with long tongs; don't forget to keep that glove handy — it's not silly.

What I do is cut a cross in the potatoes and squeeze them a little so the opening spreads and put butter in — I put plenty, it's up to you — depends on your cholesterol count ... if you believe in all that!! *See picture on page 2.*

LUCIO'S
ITALIAN RESTAURANT

Salad of Wild Mushrooms and Barbecued Figs

Ingredients for 4 people

For the marinade
2 tblspns good quality wine vinegar
1/2 cup virgin olive oil
1/2 lemon, squeezed
crushed garlic
chives, chopped
fresh thyme

12 fresh figs
2 bunches of watercress, washed and excess stalks removed
200 gm shitake mushrooms, roughly sliced

For the dressing
extra virgin olive oil
white wine vinegar
salt and pepper

Mix all marinade ingredients together in a bowl. Slice figs in half lengthwise and place in marinade for about 2 hours.

Grill figs and mushrooms on the BBQ very quickly. Put watercress and mushrooms in a salad bowl with dressing.

To serve: Mound cress and mushroom mix in centre of plate, arrange hot fig halves (cut side up) around it. Sprinkle on ground pepper and serve immediately.

This salad can be enjoyed as an entree while waiting for the main BBQ to cook, or as a side dish.

This recipe courtesy of Lucio's Italian Restaurant, Paddington, NSW.

Sweet Potato Chips —
A Barbecue Treat

1. Slice sweet potato thinly — about 3 mm thick. (Peeling is optional.)
2. Place slices on lightly oiled BBQ plate, with low to moderate heat.
3. Cook until browned and crisp by turning occasionally. (More serious connoisseurs will prefer to microwave slices first for 1-minute on HIGH to retain more flavour and colour in their chips.)
4. Salt to taste.

The above is from the Tweed Fruit & Vegetable Growers' Association Inc, Kingscliff, NSW.

Barbecued Mushrooms

whole flat or large cup mushrooms
butter
salt and pepper to taste

1. Place mushrooms, stalk-side up, on a lightly oiled
hot plate. Top with butter and sprinkle with salt and
pepper to taste.
2. Cook for about 8 minutes without turning.

Barbecued Whole Tomatoes

Serves 4
4 large tomatoes, halved
2 tablespoons oil
salt and pepper to taste
4 fresh basil leaves

1. Brush the tomato halves with oil and sprinkle with
salt and pepper to taste. Place 1 basil leaf on the
bottom half of the tomato and replace the top half.
Wrap in heavy duty foil.
2. Barbecue over medium/low heat for 25-30 minutes.

Barbecued Onions

Serves 4
1 tablespoon oil
2 large onions, cut into thick rings
salt and pepper to taste
pinch sugar

1. Brush hot plate with oil and allow to heat. Add the
onions and cook turning often for about 15-20 minutes
until golden brown and cooked through. Season to taste
with salt, pepper and sugar.

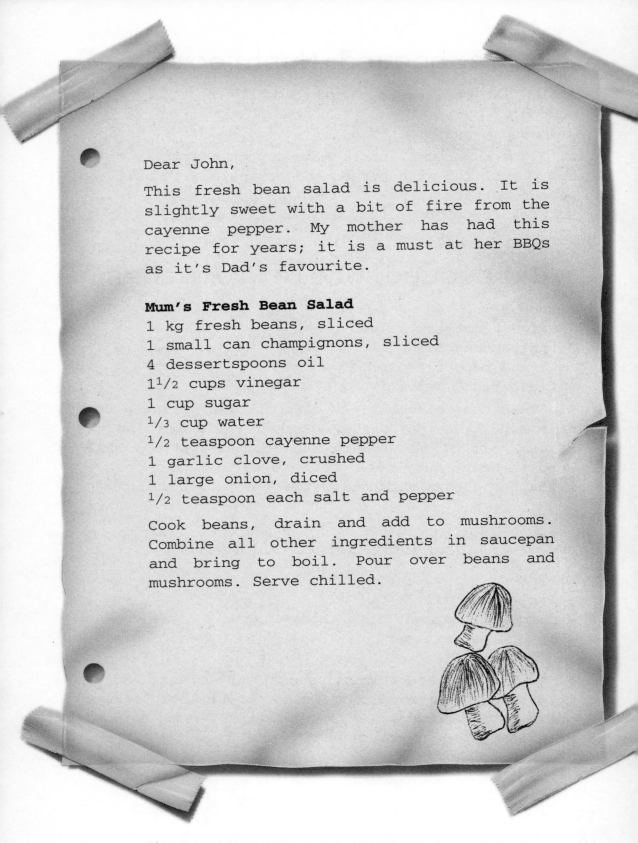

Dear John,

This fresh bean salad is delicious. It is slightly sweet with a bit of fire from the cayenne pepper. My mother has had this recipe for years; it is a must at her BBQs as it's Dad's favourite.

Mum's Fresh Bean Salad

1 kg fresh beans, sliced
1 small can champignons, sliced
4 dessertspoons oil
1^1/$_2$ cups vinegar
1 cup sugar
^{1}/$_3$ cup water
^{1}/$_2$ teaspoon cayenne pepper
1 garlic clove, crushed
1 large onion, diced
^{1}/$_2$ teaspoon each salt and pepper

Cook beans, drain and add to mushrooms. Combine all other ingredients in saucepan and bring to boil. Pour over beans and mushrooms. Serve chilled.

This recipe and illustration are from Lyn Irvine, Kempsey, NSW.

Coleslaw

Serves 4-6
$1/2$ savoy cabbage, shredded
2 large carrots, grated
1 stalk celery, finely sliced
1 large apple, cored and finely diced
425 g can crushed pineapple, drained
$3/4$ cup sour cream
$1/4$ cup whole egg mayonnaise
1 tablespoon mild mustard
1 tablespoon lemon juice
salt and pepper to taste

1. Combine the cabbage, carrots, celery, apple and pineapple in a large bowl.
2. In another bowl, combine the sour cream, mayonnaise, mustard, lemon juice and salt and pepper to taste.
2. Toss through cabbage mixture and serve immediately.

Potato Salad

Serves 4
750 g baby new potatoes
$1/2$ cup sour cream
$1/4$ cup mayonnaise
2 shallots, finely chopped
1 clove garlic, crushed
1 tablespoon lemon juice
2 tablespoons snipped fresh chives

1. Boil potatoes until tender. Drain and plunge into ice cold water to stop the cooking process. Drain again.
2. Combine the sour cream, mayonnaise, shallots, garlic and lemon juice and mix well. Pour over the potatoes and toss well to coat. Serve sprinkled with chives.

Barbecued Sweet Corn

For as long as I can remember I've loved corn on the cob but I've loathed cooking it — having to get a huge pot of water, wait for it to come to the boil, toss in maybe six or eight cobs of corn (which of course immediately takes it off the boil) then wait for it to come back to the boil — all the fussing and draining, it was all just too much effort. Being one who likes to reduce the amount of effort required in any cooking, I decided I would try barbecuing them. The result, I think, is just wonderful.

Leave corn in the husk and cook them if you want to. That's the lazy way. It's better to peel the husk back — but don't remove it — and get rid of all that hairy stuff inside, then replace the husk. Soak the corn in cold water for 5-10 minutes, take out, and place above medium to hot coals, turning often. When the husks are dark brown (that will probably take about 12-15 minutes) take them off, remove the husk, bang on the butter, lots of ground pepper and off you go.

Incidentally, if you bought them in a package where the husks have been removed, simply put the sweet corn on the barbecue without any real worries. In fact, I often like it better this way because the outside can get a little charred. It looks good, and it seems to taste sweeter for some reason.

See picture on page 127.

CHEESE AND WINE

I believe that if you possibly can, you should make the barbecue a complete meal. Many tend to do a steak, maybe some potatoes, a little salad, and that's the meal. I think the barbecue deserves a lot more consideration than this, given that some of the recipes in the book are quite sophisticated. I do think it's worth your while to finish up with some good Australian cheese on crackers or crunchy bread — and a good bottle of wine, if you feel inclined.

We create some of the most wonderful cheeses in the world in Australia so don't fall for this nonsense of having to have French Brie, or Italian this, or European that. You just can't beat Australian cheese. I have a friend, Andrew Strachan, who knows a lot about wines and a lot about cheese. Andrew has Kims, the Beachside Retreat at Toowoon Bay in New South Wales and Andrew is a lover of all things that can be considered the best. He and I have talked quite a lot about cheese.

Some recommendations follow — bear in mind that some of them may be a little hard to find, but make an effort because cheese to finish off a barbecue makes it really complete and it's not as though it requires much. I prefer it with crunchy bread to biscuits, but it's up to you.

I recently had the opportunity to enjoy a whole new range of cheeses from the Hunter Valley. Andrew and I are yet to enjoy these together and I'm telling you these are the cheeses to watch. They are all created in the one small factory that, I suspect somehow, will become one big factory. After you've tasted some of these cheeses I think you might agree. The one slight problem is there might be, at this stage, some difficulty in obtaining these cheeses.

Kims

BEACHSIDE RETREAT

TOOWOON BAY: 33°21'.45 SOUTH, 151°30'.0 EAST.

Dear John,
These are the cheeses you and I
have enjoyed and talked about
in the past. I hope they are of
some benefit to what, I am sure,
will be a brilliant cookbook.
I look forward to celebrating
its success with you, hopefully
here at Kims.
Kind regards,
Andrew Strachan

AUSTRALIAN CHEESES

ADMIRALTY BLUE - King Island

A traditional English style cheese with a natural rind and a rich creamy interior.

BASS RIVER RED - Bena, Victoria

A whole milk semi hard cheese (waxed barrel).

Cheesemaker: Fred Lappin

CAPRICORN GOAT CAMEMBERT - Woodside, South Australia

A white mould goats milk cheese.

Cheesemaker: Paula Jenkins

CYGNET RIVER HALOUMI - Gum Creek Road, Kangaroo Island, South Australia

A pure sheep's milk cheese made to a recipe originating from Cyprus.

Cheesemaker: Susan Berlin

GIPPSLAND BLUE - Tarago River, Victoria

A whole milk cheese made with a gorgonzola mould.

Cheesemaker: Laurie Jensen

HEIDI GRUYERE - Exton, Tasmania

A natural, cow's milk cheese (Good Living, Best Cheese Award).

Cheesemaker: Frank and Elizabeth Marchand

HERMANN'S SMOKEHOUSE - Timboon, Victoria

A whole milk cheese with a natural smoked subtle flavour of a Murray River Red Gum.

Cheesemaker: Hermann Schulz

HUNTER VALLEY GOLD - Pokolbin, New South Wales

A full flavoured cows milk cheese with a soft washed rind.

Cheesemaker: Peter Curtis

JINDI BRIE - Jindivick, Victoria

A white mould traditional brie (World Champion Soft Cheese USA).

Cheesemaker: Craig Sceney

KANGAROO ISLAND BRIE - Penneshaw, Kangaroo Island, South Australia

A surface ripened cheese made from full cream milk with no stabiliser or preservatives added.

Cheesemaker: Moss and Liz Howard

BEACHSIDE RETREAT *Kims*

TOOWOON BAY: 33°21' .45 SOUTH, 151°30'.0 EAST.

KING ISLAND CHEDDAR - *King Island, Tasmania*

A full flavoured open textured cheddar matured for a minimum of twelve months.

MARGARET RIVER BRIE - *Western Australia*

An extremely rich cheese which has been brine dipped and allowed to ripen naturally.

MEREDITH ROQUEFORT STYLE - *Victoria*

A pure sheeps milk blue cheese similar to a traditional Roquefort.

Cheesemaker: Sandy Cameron

MILAWA BLUE - *Milawa, Victoria*

A soft blue cheese with a mild flavour enhanced by a delicate green/white mould.

Cheesemaker: George Letchford

MOUNT BUFFALO BLUE - *Milawa, Victoria*

A pure goats milk cheese with distinctive sharp flavour (Australian Dairy Association Gold Medal).

Cheesemaker: David Brown

MOUNT EMU CREEK MATURED - *Camperdown, Victoria.*

A cloth bound semi pressed ewe milk cheese matured for nine months (Champion Royal Agricultural Show).

Cheesemaker: John Staaks

PHOQUES COVE CAMEMBERT - *King Island*

A soft, surface ripened, white mould cheese (Champion Cheese Royal Agricultural Show).

PYPNGANA CHEDDAR - *Pypngana, Tasmania*

The best example of a traditional cloth bound aged cheddar.

Cheesemaker: John Healey

TOP PADDOCK WASHED RIND - *Bena, Victoria*

A soft creamy (port salut style) washed rind cheese.

Cheesemaker: Fred Leppin

TIMBOON CAMEMBERT - *Ford and Fells Road, Timboon, Victoria*

Award winning cheese made from their own biodynamic farm milk using traditional methods.

Cheesemaker: Hermann Schulz

WAUCHOPE GLOUCESTER - *Wauchope, New South Wales*

Named after the famous United Kingdom cheeses, Double and Single Gloucester. This very tasty matured cheese is made by the Hasting Cooperative from rich fresh local milk.

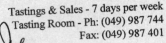

Dear John, I know you like our Hunter Cheese; & although you sampled some over lunch the other day I thought you might like some more for a review. With best wishes - Brian Neli.

HUNTER VALLEY BIANCO

Something different to tempt you! Hunter Valley Bianco is an unripened 100% Cows mild curd cheese. The flavour and texture being similar to the Italian boccincini (young mozzarella) which makes it ideal to serve in salads and luncheon dishes combining tomato, basil, green peppercorns and a light balsamic vinigarette. A truly versatile cheese.

FROMAGE BLANC

A true farmhouse fresh curd cheese with an appealing acid character. It has a creamy texture and slightly citrus after taste. Made from 100% Sheep's milk it covers the sweet and savoury food range with ease. We suggest Fromage Blanc with fresh fruit for a stunning weekend brunch. Small rounds of Fromage Blanc atop pastrami or ham, pickles and dark rye bread or a grand finale to a superb dinner-Fromage Blanc blended with double cream, figs in syrup and dusted with demerara sugar prettily arranged on dinner sized plates.

HUNTER VALLEY CHEVRE

Made from 100% Goats Milk and well entrenched in the homes and eateries of Europe this fresh white cheese is fast gaining favour in Australia. Chevre is ideally suited to marinating or cooking as it holds its shape under high heat. We suggest a tempting Hunter Valley Goats cheese salad, focaccia with goats cheese, finely sliced roasted and peeled red pepper, cracked black peppercorns drizzled with excellent quality virgin olive oil or gourmet pizza of leeks, artichoke hearts and chevre. Hunter Valley Chevre also available blended with fresh herbs.

HUNTER VALLEY TABLE CHEVRE

Central to any dinner party cheese platter is a focus, something new and different to tempt the tastebuds. Hunter Valley Table Chevre is ideal for this situation, or enjoy it just for yourself. Made from 100% pure Goats milk this delicate white moulded pyramid is aged up to six weeks. Once mature, the texture and flavour progresses as it ages ranging from firm and delicate to creamy with strong goat flavour at maximum maturation. Allowing you to serve this cheese exactly at your preferred age.

HUNTER VALLEY AGED ASHED CHEVRE

The French are masters at the tradition of goats cheese manufacture, following in this tradition Hunter Valley Aged Ashed Chevre combines the craft of cheesemaking with the skill of food preservation. Made from 100% pure goats milk this table size pyramid of chevre is dusted with grape vine ash, white moulded, aged up to four weeks and results in a fine textured chevre with enhanced goat flavour.

BRANXTON BRIE

Home of our cheesemaker and a tribute to the perseverance of our early Hunter Valley winemakers.

Branxton Brie is lovingly made, a little capricious in maturation and suffers only the gentlest handling. The results speak for themselves, a delightful round of white mould cheese with a deliciously soft and creamy interior.

HUNTER VALLEY GOLD WASHED RIND

A firm favourite and a great introduction to the washed rind cheese style. Washed Rind as a cheese variety has a long history and can readily be found in the provincial markets of France where local producers vend their produce weekly, selling or bartering for other essential household staples.

Hunter Valley Gold Washed Rind is a subtle flavoured cheese, ideal for snacks or gourmet cheese platters. Wonderful served with fresh crusty bread or damper, it can be eaten at various stages of its maturity.

POKOLBIN GOLD

A cheese with Heart!!

Pokolbin Gold has a robust, yeasty flavour and possesses a pungency and strength not often found in Australian cheese. This cheese is at home with the likes of Port Salut, Munster and Pont l'Eveque. One for the connoisseur.

POKOLBIN WHITE

A fresh acid cheese with a delicate yeasty flavour. It marries well with champagne and most of our local Hunter Valley wines. Aged for 3 to 4 months, this cheese is a delightful alternative to cheddar on your cheese plate.

CESSNOCK CHEDDAR

Cheesemakers Selection. A very special addition to our range. Cessnock Cheddar is a handmade Australian Cheddar, a rarity is these days of mass production and high tech preservation techniques. A 3 kg wheel of classic cheddar, as opposed to a block, it is cloth bound and waxed to produce what is known as 'Rind on Cheddar'. Aged to its maximum potential, this cheese has been selected and named to match the full bodied wines of the Pokolbin Valley.

BUSBY BLUE

An assertive blue vein cheese for the true cheese lover. A flavoursome blue bite is enhanced by the addition of pure cream for an overall taste sensation. A must on your mixed cheese platter or perhaps a minimalistic gourmet platter of blue cheese and fresh pears served with good quality breads.

Named for James Busby, an early Hunter Valley pioneer (1825) with an all embracing passion for viticulture. We hope this cheese will do him honour, we feel sure he would approve.

POKOLBIN CLUB BLUE

Cheesemakers Selection. A blend of cheeses, aged whites and blues of varying strengths and textures combining to achieve a pressed block of delightful blue vein cheese. Particularly useful for catering.

As good cheeses are considered important, by me, to the perfect barbecue, so are good wines. Obviously, I have strong allegiance with the Rosemount organisation and with the Oatley family who, I am proud to say, are dear and close friends of mine, as is Chris Hancock who has been responsible for the success of Rosemount wine sales all over the world.

Rosemount is one of our great exporters of wine and for one reason only: they are one of our great creators of wine. They also happen to produce and distribute my own wine that we call Cloud Valley. Philip Shaw, whom I'll talk about later, created our Cloud Valley Sauvignon Blanc and our Cloud Valley Semillon, both particularly high quality although mid-range priced wines that you might like to try.

Don't be swept up by the nonsense that we need to have wines from overseas. I believe there is only one that we need to buy from overseas, as we can't create it here, and that is champagne.

If you lean towards the luxury of French champagne before or after your barbecue, then allow me to recommend the champagne created by another friend of mine, Monsieur Nicholas Feuillate. French champagne, as you know, is not cheap, however, if there is a special reason for a special barbecue, and a barbecue can be quite a formal affair, then do try this one created by my friend.

As far as wines are concerned, our wines compare with the best in the world and some, in fact, are officially recognised as the best in the world according to astute overseas' judges.

As a measure of Australia's lofty standing in the world of wine, our best known drop, Penfolds Grange, now carries the accolade of "international wine of the year" from the influential American wine bible, *Wine Spectator*, and wines from my very good friends at Rosemount Estate in the Hunter Valley — like Roxburgh Chardonnay and Balmoral Syrah — have also achieved stunning success in important overseas judgings against the best wines in the world.

Dollar for dollar and glass for glass, Australian wine represents an exciting challenge to all wine-producing countries, as evidenced by the dramatic increase in wine exports in the past decade. What's really pleasing is that it's now possible to enjoy our premium wines in the finest restaurants in London, New York, Paris and Hong Kong, aboard the world's top ocean liners and in the cabins of international airlines.

As you may have guessed, I'm a particularly big fan of Hunter Wines, especially those superbly crafted by Rosemount's talented custodian Philip Shaw, who includes the ranking of "international winemaker of the year" in his many credits. The Hunter is best known for its chardonnays and semillons and for reds made from its traditional red grape, Shiraz.

Flamboyant Brian McGuigan is another fastidious Hunter winemaker and names like Drayton, Tulloch and Tyrrell enjoy legendary status throughout the Valley.

Other prominent NSW wine-producing regions are Griffith (home of De Bortoli's outstanding dessert wine, Noble One), Mudgee, Cowra (a booming Chardonnay district), Orange and even the Snowy Mountains. Yes, that's right, we now even make wine from grapes grown in the foothills of the Snowy Mountains at Tumbarumba.

The dozen or so wineries in the Canberra district are also becoming a force in their own, small way. Chardonnays and rieslings from companies like Helms are well worth tracking down.

In Victoria, the Yarra Valley has taken on a new lease of life since the 1980's thanks to the emergence of labels like Coldstream Hills, Yarra Ridge and the spectacular sparkling wine complex Domaine Chandon, an offshoot of France's Epernay-headquartered Möet et Chandon.

Tasmania has emerged as another trendy cool-climate area, thanks to the commendable efforts of wineries like Heemskerk and Piper's Brook and a particularly pleasing fizz called Jansz, which benefits from the input of another noted French champagne producer, Louis Roederer.

Of course, South Australia is one of our traditional wine-producing States. Reds and whites from the Barossa Valley, Clare Valley, McLaren Vale, Coonawarra, Adelaide Hills and Langhorne Creek have consistently proved themselves to be in world class. From delicate cool-climate chardonnays, sauvignon blancs and rieslings made in the Adelaide Hills by skilled technicians like Brian Croser, to booming reds made at the historic triple-gabled winery Wynns in the heart of Coonawarra, South Australia produces an exciting, versatile range of wines.

In Western Australia, the pioneering Swan Valley-based wineries Sandalford and Houghton are still going great guns, while in the south, at spectacular Margaret River, high fliers like Leeuwin Estate, Cape Mentelle and Cullens are responsible for some really marvellous chardonnays and cabernets.

In spite of the difficulties involved in growing grapes in hot climates, winemakers in Queensland's Granite Belt have not been deterred one bit. Look out for labels such as Ballandean Estate and Robinson's Family and I bet you'll be pleasantly surprised.

All up, there are more than 750 wine producers — some large, many small — spread throughout Australia and all are doing an exceptional job in raising the standard of our wines and delivering superb enjoyment to a rapidly-growing army of admirers.

INDEX

BARBECUES AVAILABLE FROM BARBEQUES GALORE

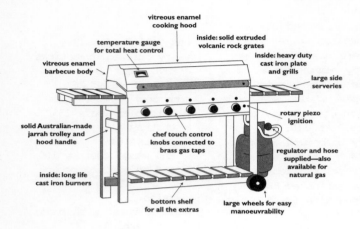

vitreous enamel
cooking hood

inside: solid extruded
volcanic rock grates

temperature gauge
for total heat control

inside: heavy duty
cast iron plate
and grills

vitreous enamel
barbecue body

large side
serveries

solid Australian-made
jarrah trolley and
hood handle

rotary piezo
ignition

chef touch control
knobs connected to
brass gas taps

regulator and hose
supplied—also
available for
natural gas

inside: long life
cast iron burners

bottom shelf
for all the extras

large wheels for easy
manoeuvrability

Dream

The deluxe of deluxe barbecues. Grill, roast or bake your taste of nostalgia on this traditional baked enamel barbecue set in an Australian jarrah trolley. The package includes a 9 kg gas cylinder with fuel gauge, a Keeping the Dream Alive apron, three piece barbecue set with long-lasting Rosewood handles, roast holder, enamel roasting dish, smoker bag, hickory chips, sauces, marinades, salad oils and dressings and a vinyl barbecue cover.

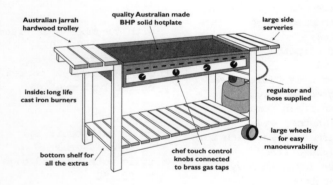

Australian jarrah
hardwood trolley

quality Australian made
BHP solid hotplate

large side
serveries

inside: long life
cast iron burners

regulator and
hose supplied

large wheels
for easy
manoeuvrability

bottom shelf for
all the extras

chef touch control
knobs connected
to brass gas taps

Knockabout

The thinking behind this design was to cater for all those groups wanting a huge cooking surface which would be ideal for club socials and large family get-togethers and parties. The large steel plate was especially manufactured to provide even heat right across its surface which means it will cook a feast for up to 60 people without fuss. The package includes a 9 kg gas cylinder with fuel gauge to monitor gas levels in the bottle, a barbecue turn to enable you to flip, cut, slice and turn the food and a Keeping the Dream Alive apron.

heavy duty
cast iron grills

heavy duty plate
with handles

internal wire
fuel rack

robust steel trolley
with wooden
side shelves

vitreous enamel
barbecue frame

extra large
ash catcher

wheels for
mobility

bottom shelf for
all the extras

Fair Dinkum 44

This barbecue was designed using the traditional Aussie half petrol drum. This vitreous enamel charcoal barbecue comes complete on a metal trolley plus grill, a Keeping the Dream Alive apron and heat beads.

20 SIZZLING HITS!

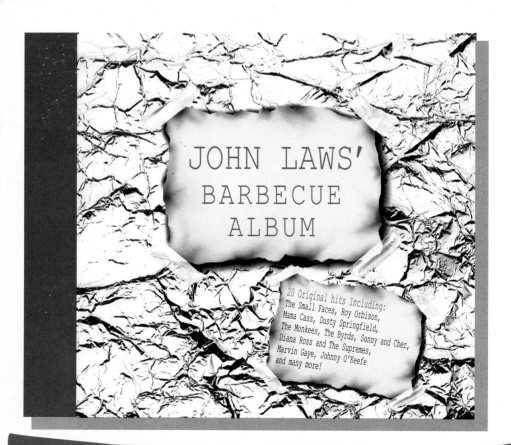

JOHN LAWS'
BARBECUE
ALBUM

20 Original hits Including:
The Small Faces, Roy Orbison,
Mama Cass, Dusty Springfield,
The Monkees, The Byrds, Sonny and Cher,
Diana Ross and The Supremes,
Marvin Gaye, Johnny O'Keefe
and many more!

To coincide with the release of his cookbook;
the John Laws' Barbecue Album. It's the perfect music
to accompany any barbecue. Enjoy this unforgettable
collection as you serve up a barbecue storm.

SONY
MUSIC

Available on C.D. and Cassette from all good record stores